Cobblestone Cats

Botanical Gardens

Buenos Aires

Panattoni

Published by:
Panattoni Press
P.O. BOX 9022381
SAN JUAN, PR 00902

www.panattoniprintshop.com

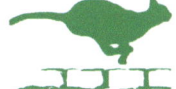

Cobblestone Cats

Cats of Botanical Gardens

The Botanical Gardens or Jardín Botánico Carlos Thays is located in the heart of the Palermo District in Buenos Aires. It is named after the French landscape architect who immigrated to Argentina in 1889 and became Buenos Aires's Director of Parks and Walkways in 1891. The triangular shaped garden, bordered by bustling city streets, was declared a national monument in 1996. It is 17.24 acres and has approximately 5,500 species of plants, shrubs and trees, as well as, a number of sculptures, greenhouses and, of course, cats.

The cats that live in the Botanical Garden roam the acreage free and friendly. As a visitor you will see cats peeking out from behind statues, strolling down a dirt path, or curled up on a park bench. The vast majority of the cats are not feral to the gardens, but abandoned domestic cats. A group of dedicated volunteers, Asociacion Civil Gatos Botanico, care for the cats and will trap, neuter and release to help control the cat population. They also find homes for the cats through their adoption program.

The Cats of the Botanical Gardens are documented through these pages · · · · · · · · · · · ·

.... Enjoy!

The Proailurus, meaning "before the cats", is believed to be the latest ancestor of all felines living around 20 million years ago

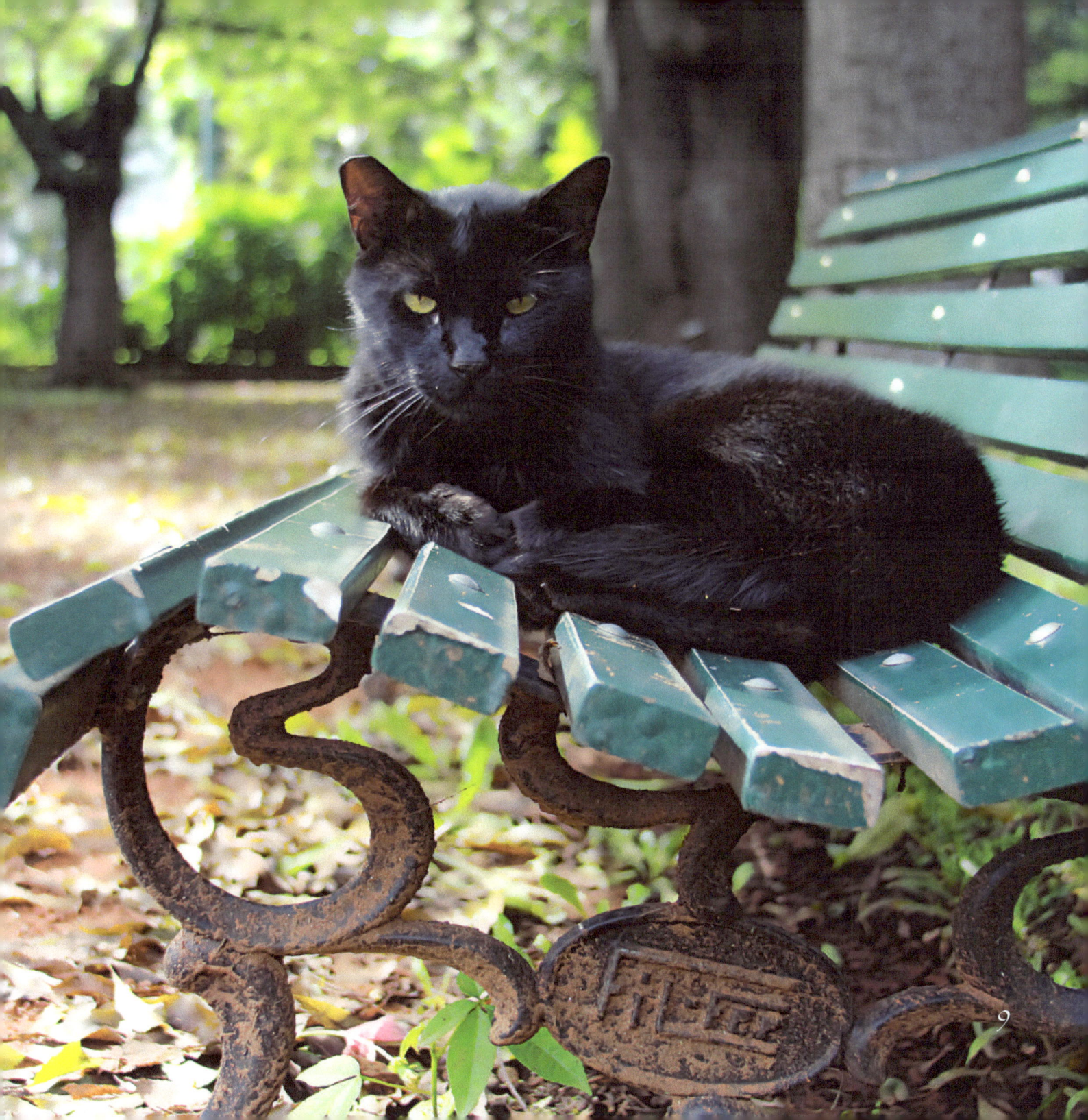

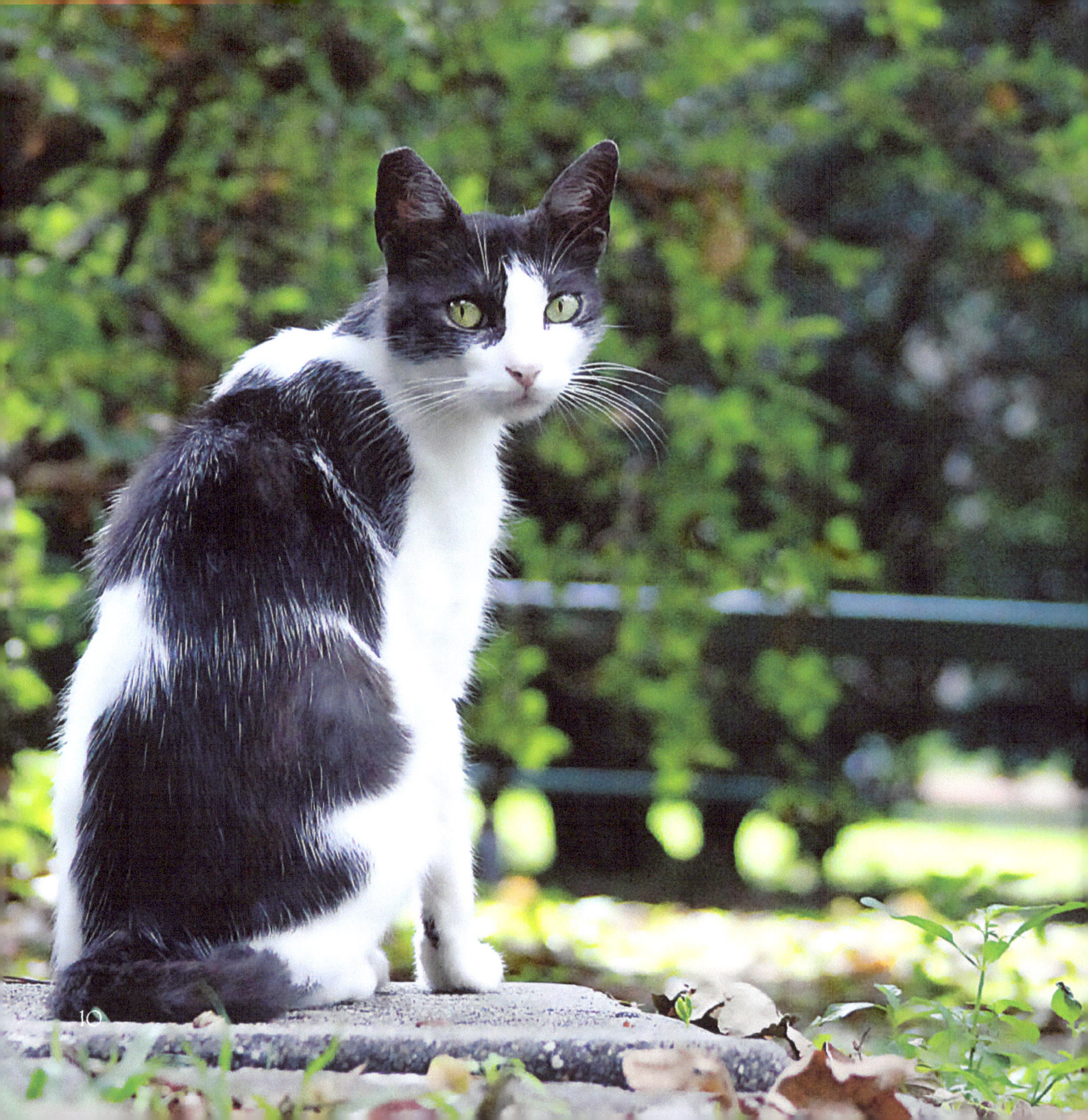

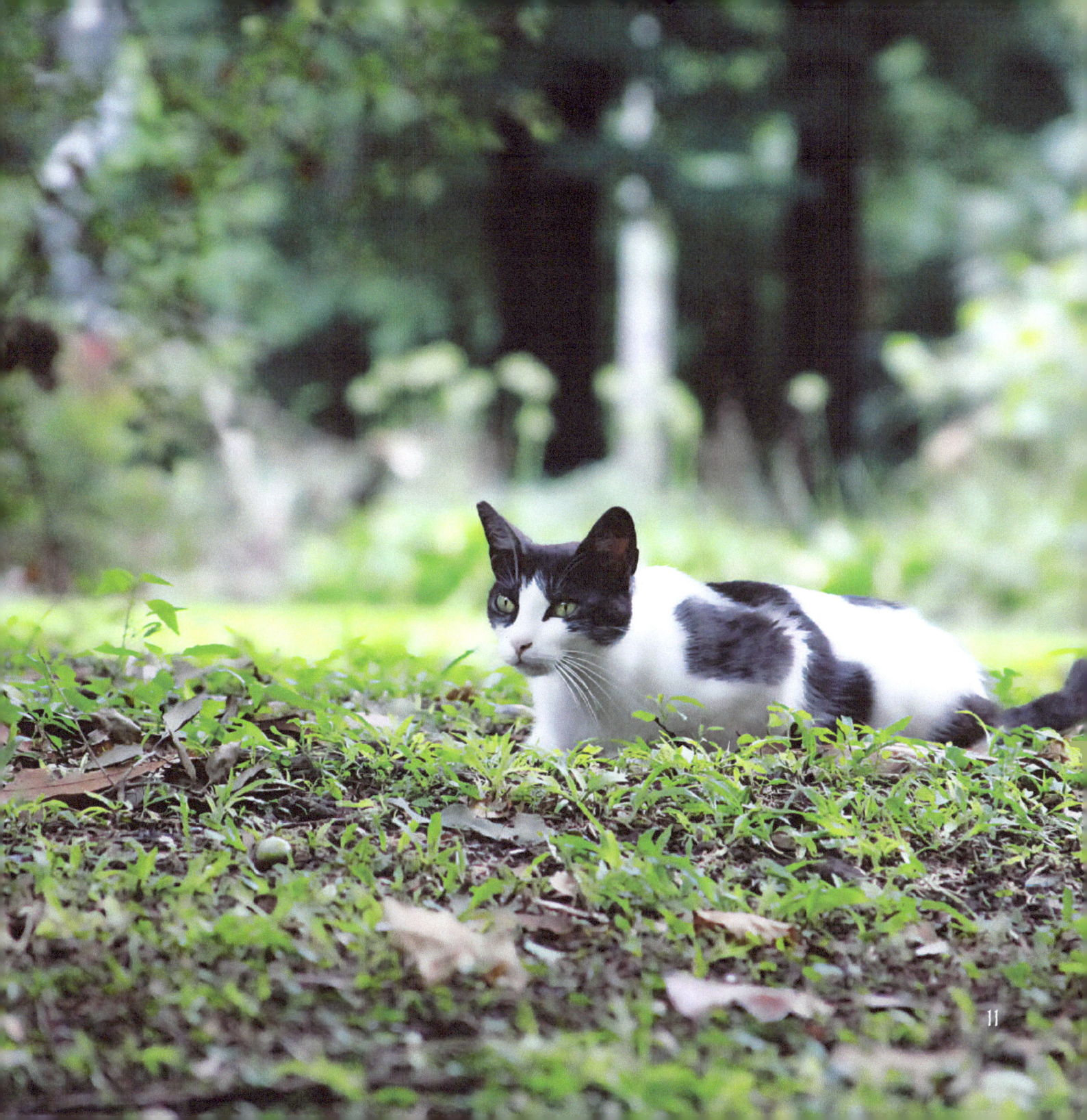

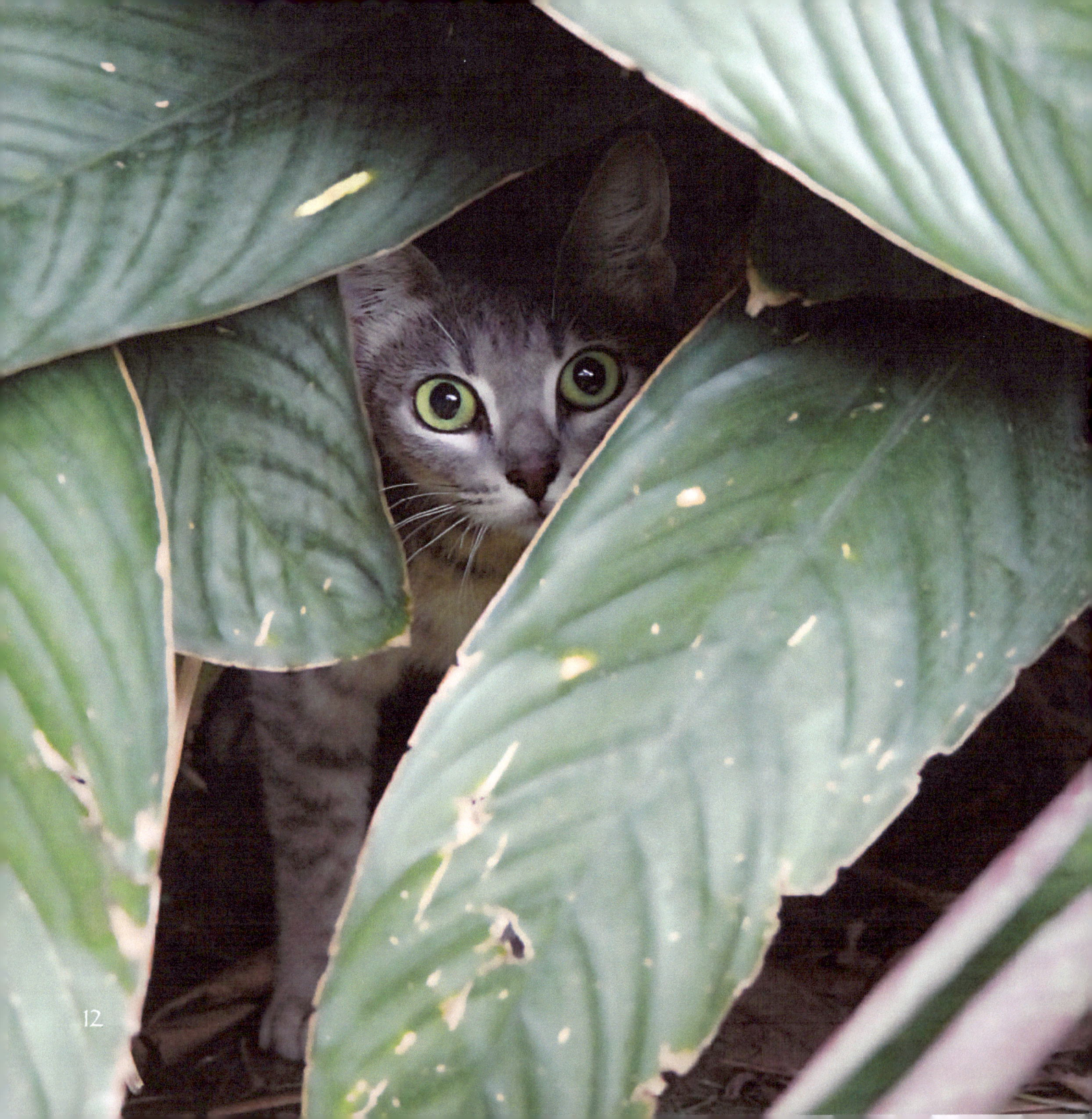

Buenos Aires is known as the "Paris of Latin America" with world-class opera, architecture, and cuisine

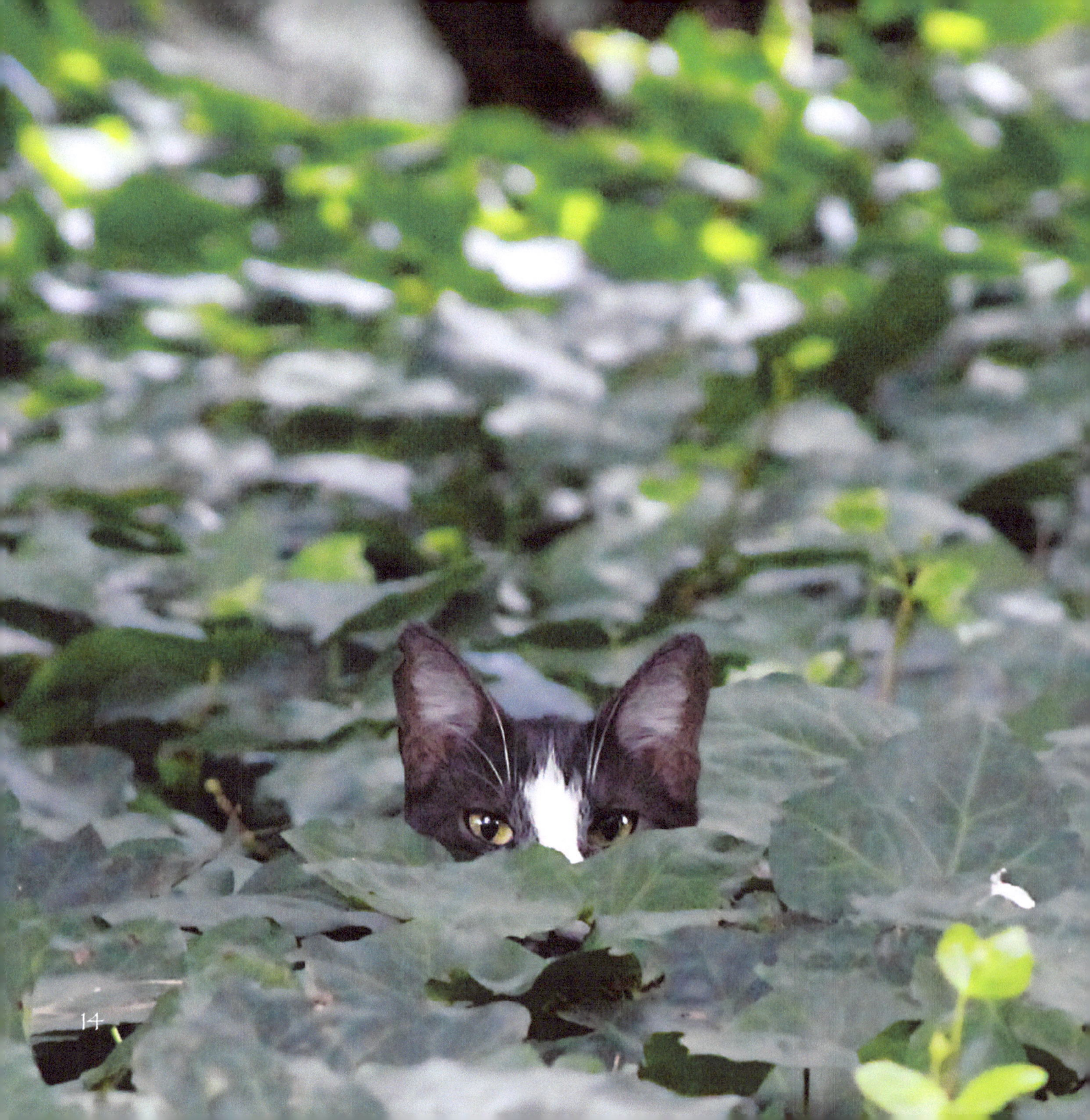

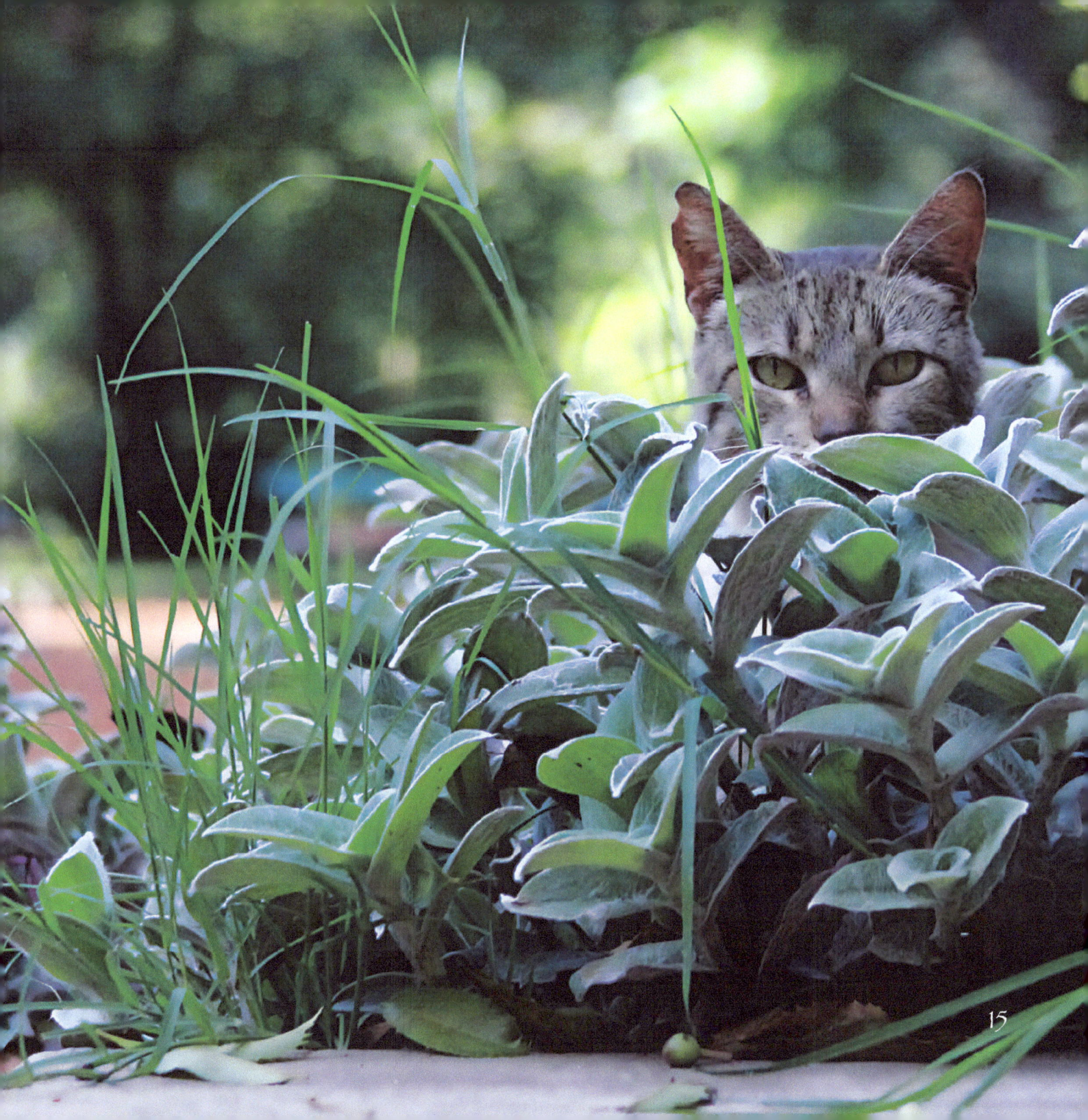

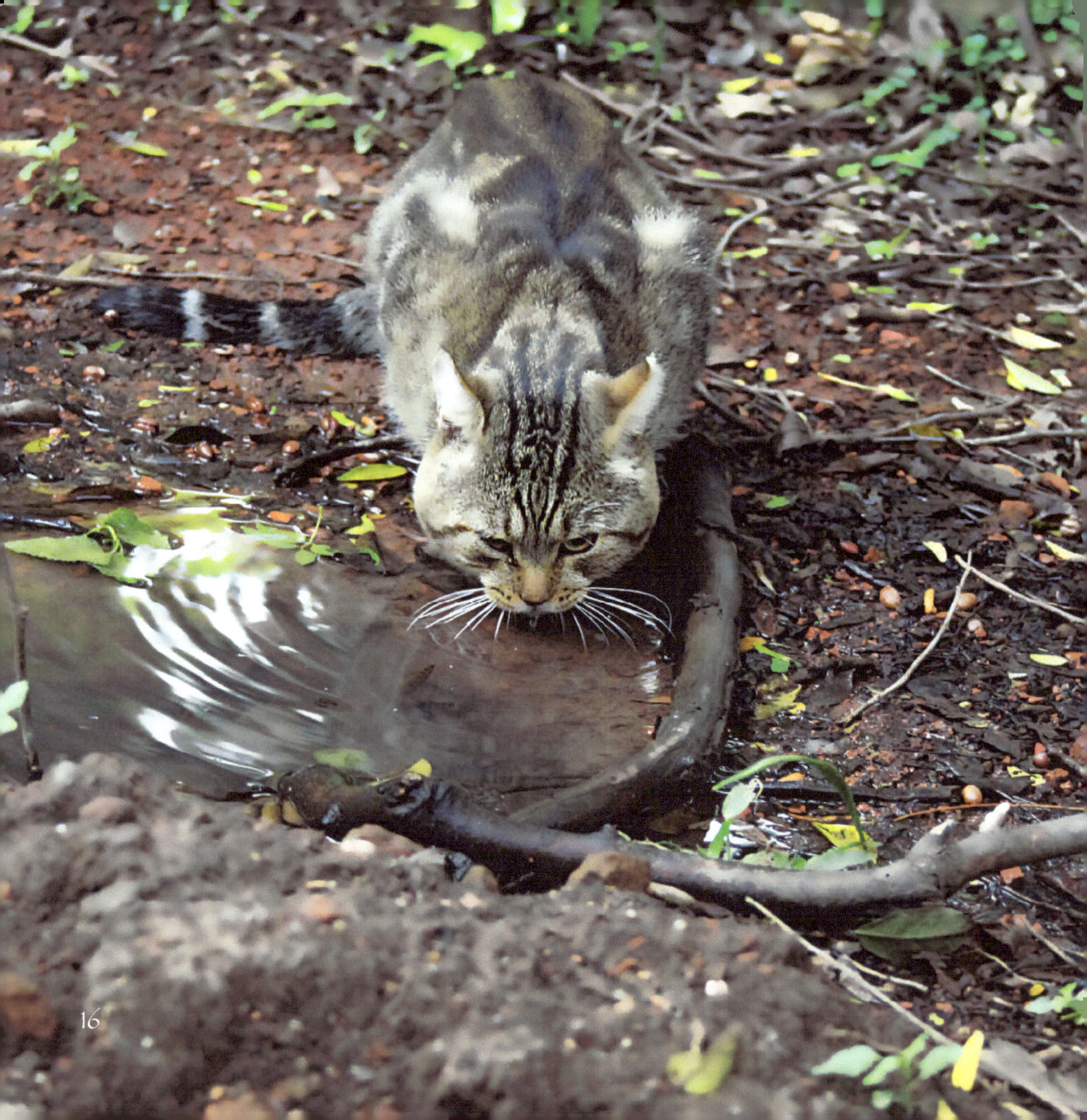

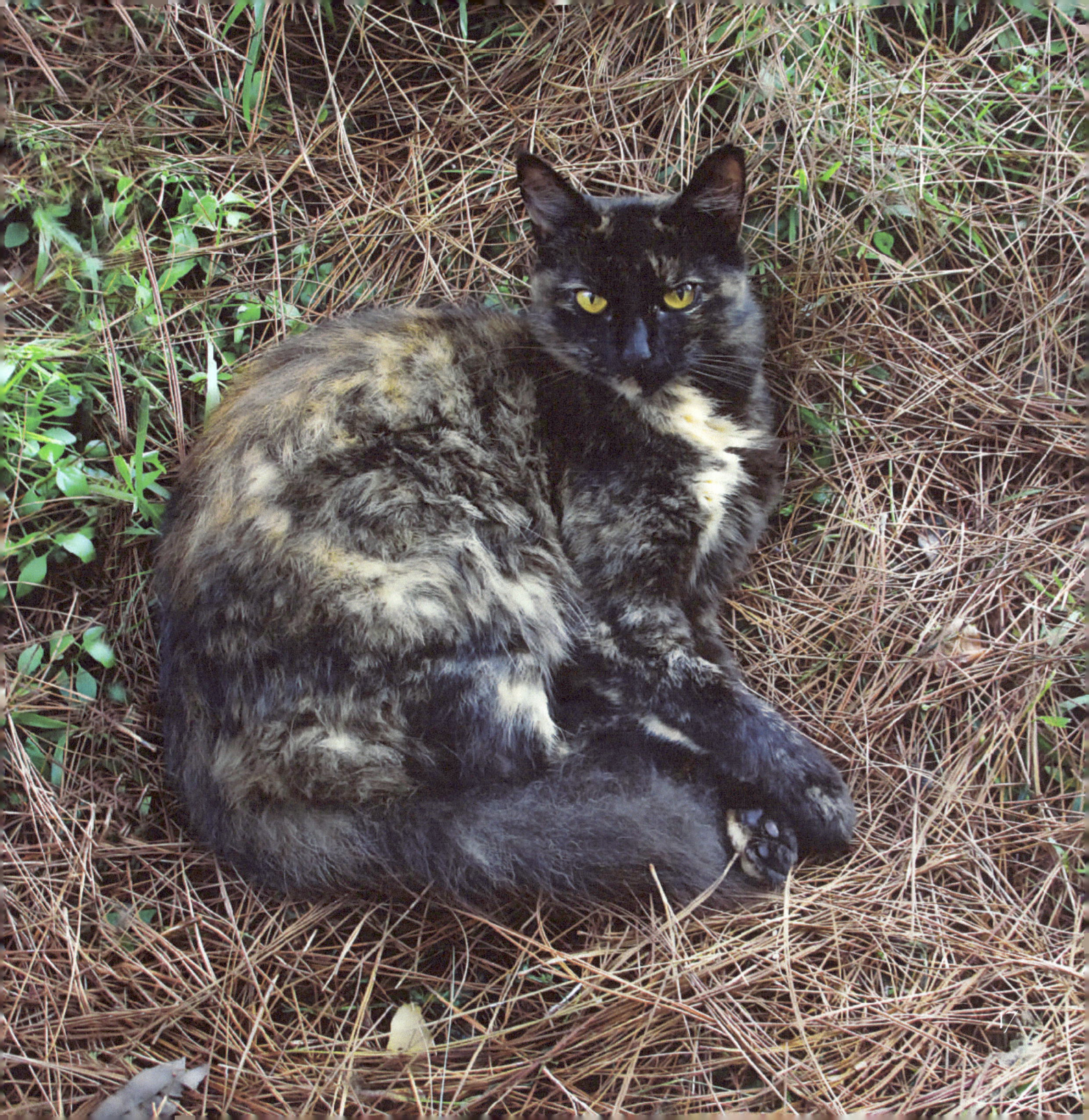

Smuggling a cat out of ancient Egypt was punishable by death

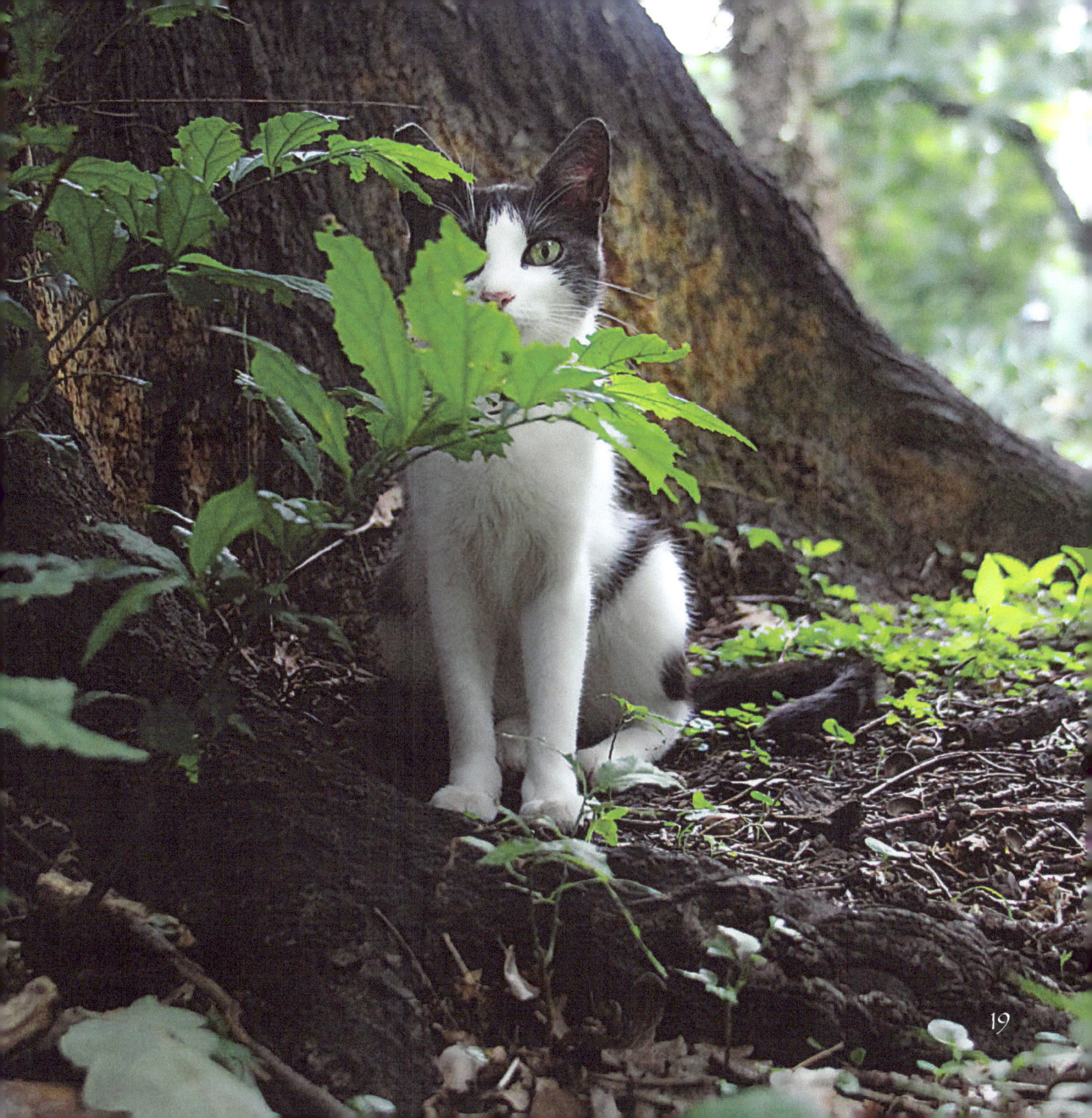

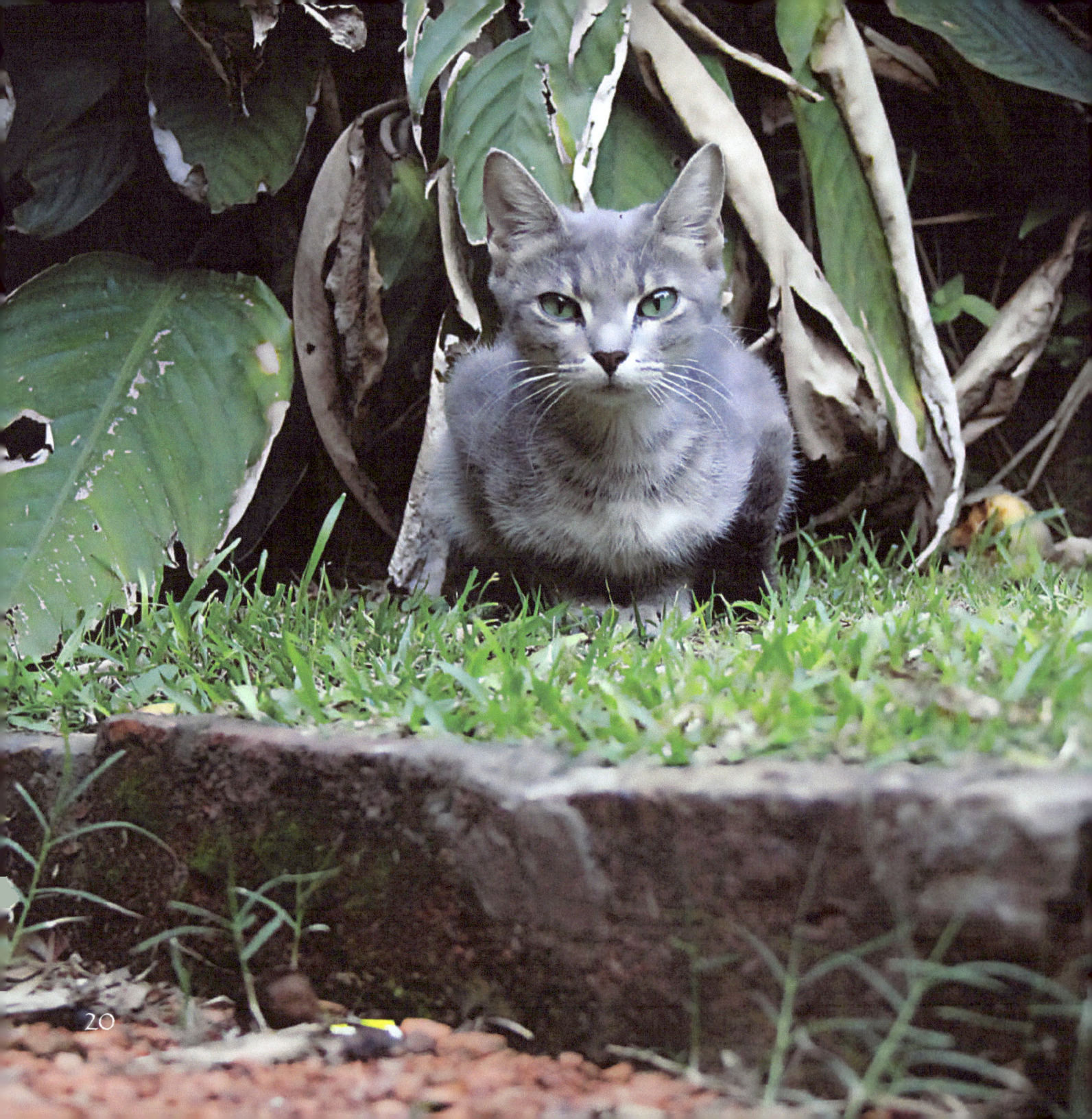

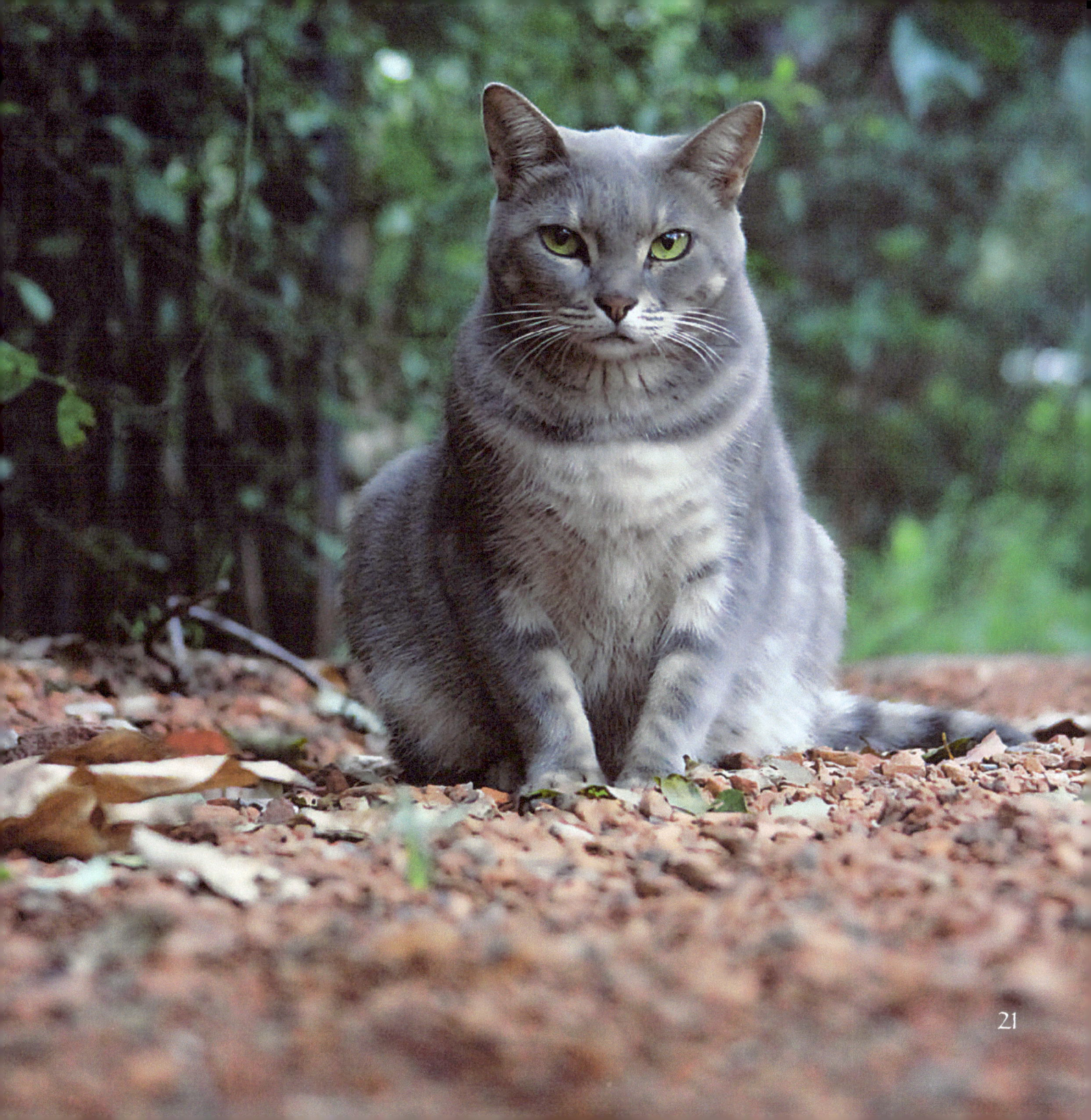

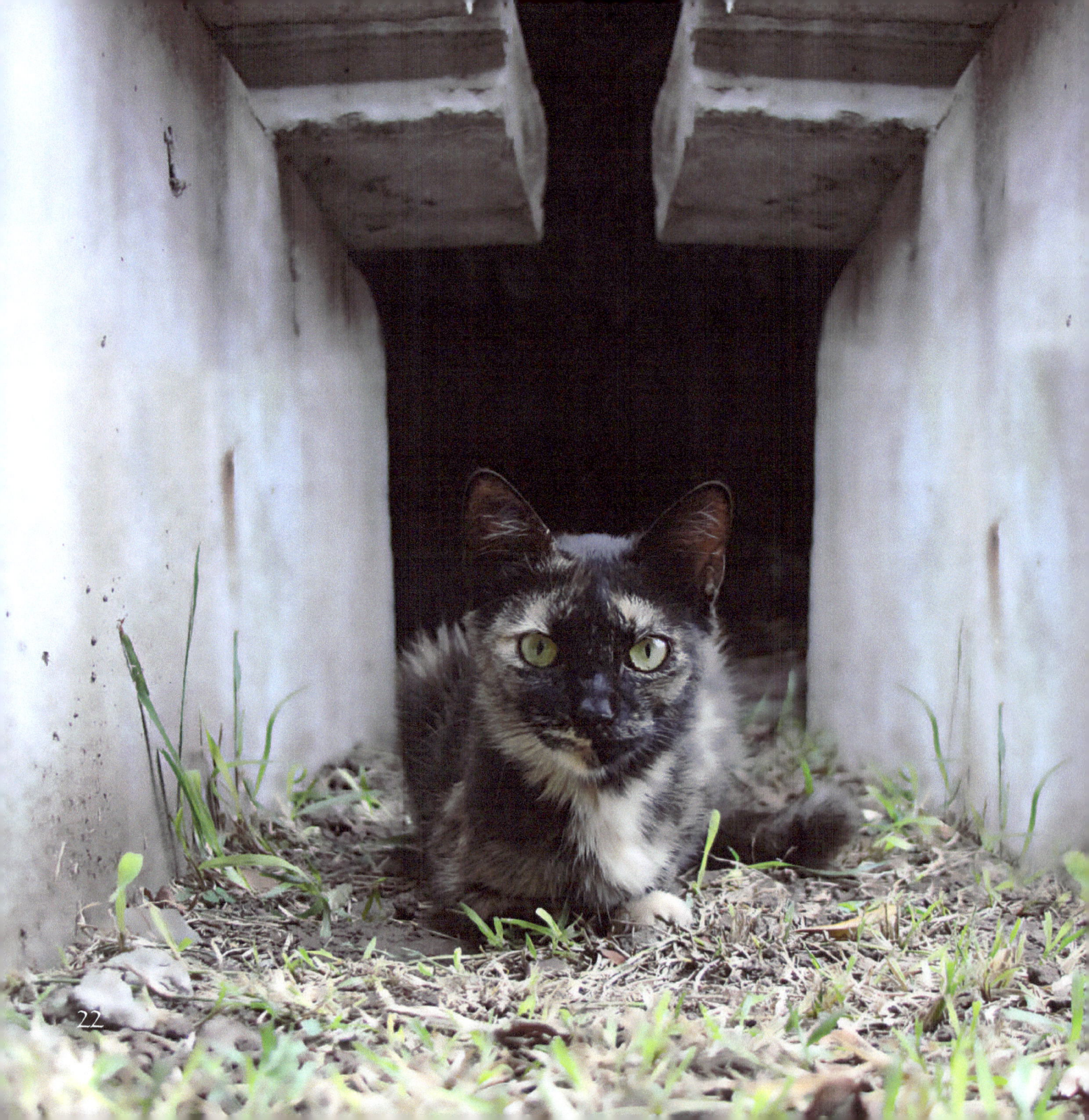

The port in Buenos Aires is the largest in all of South America

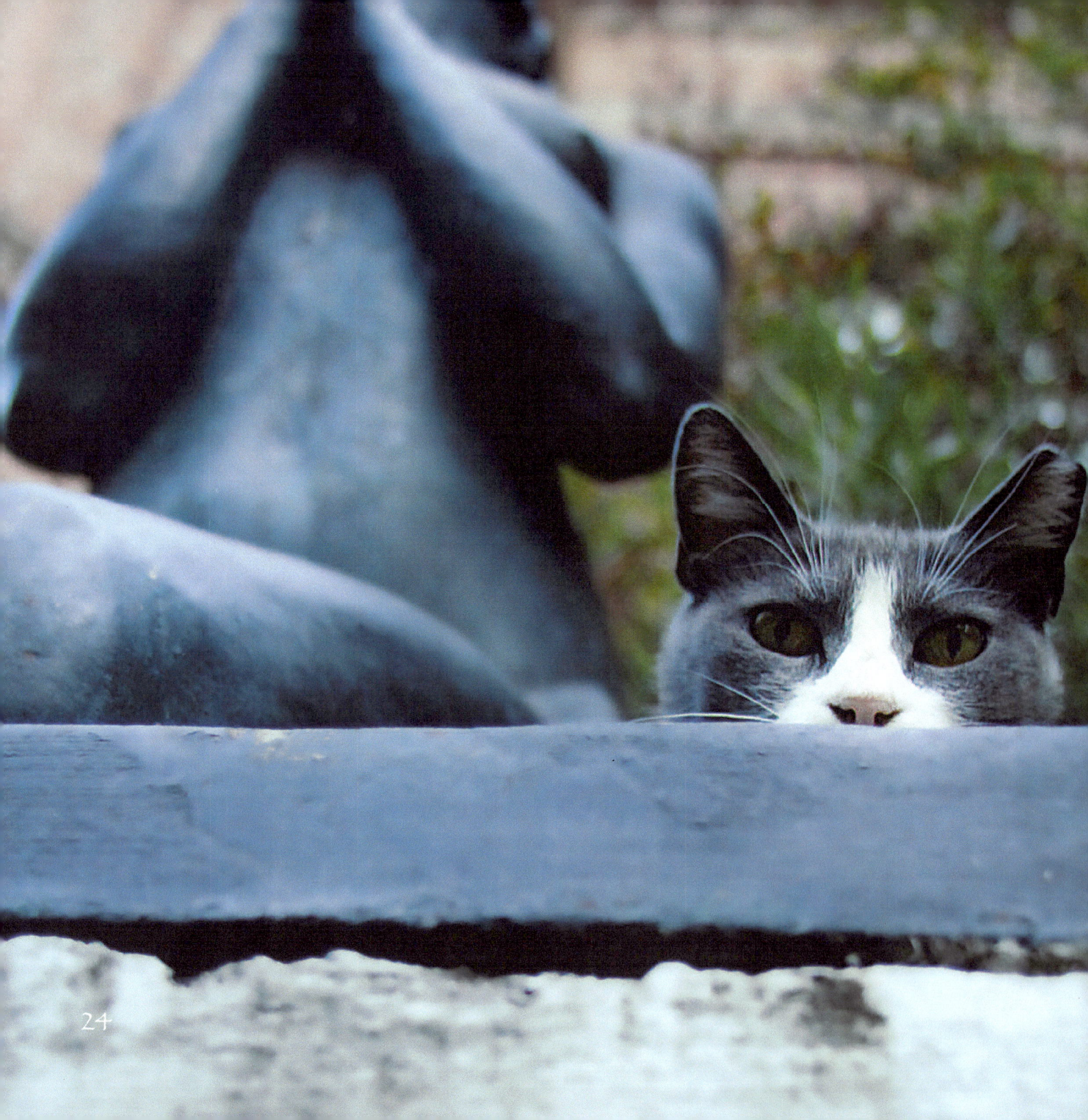

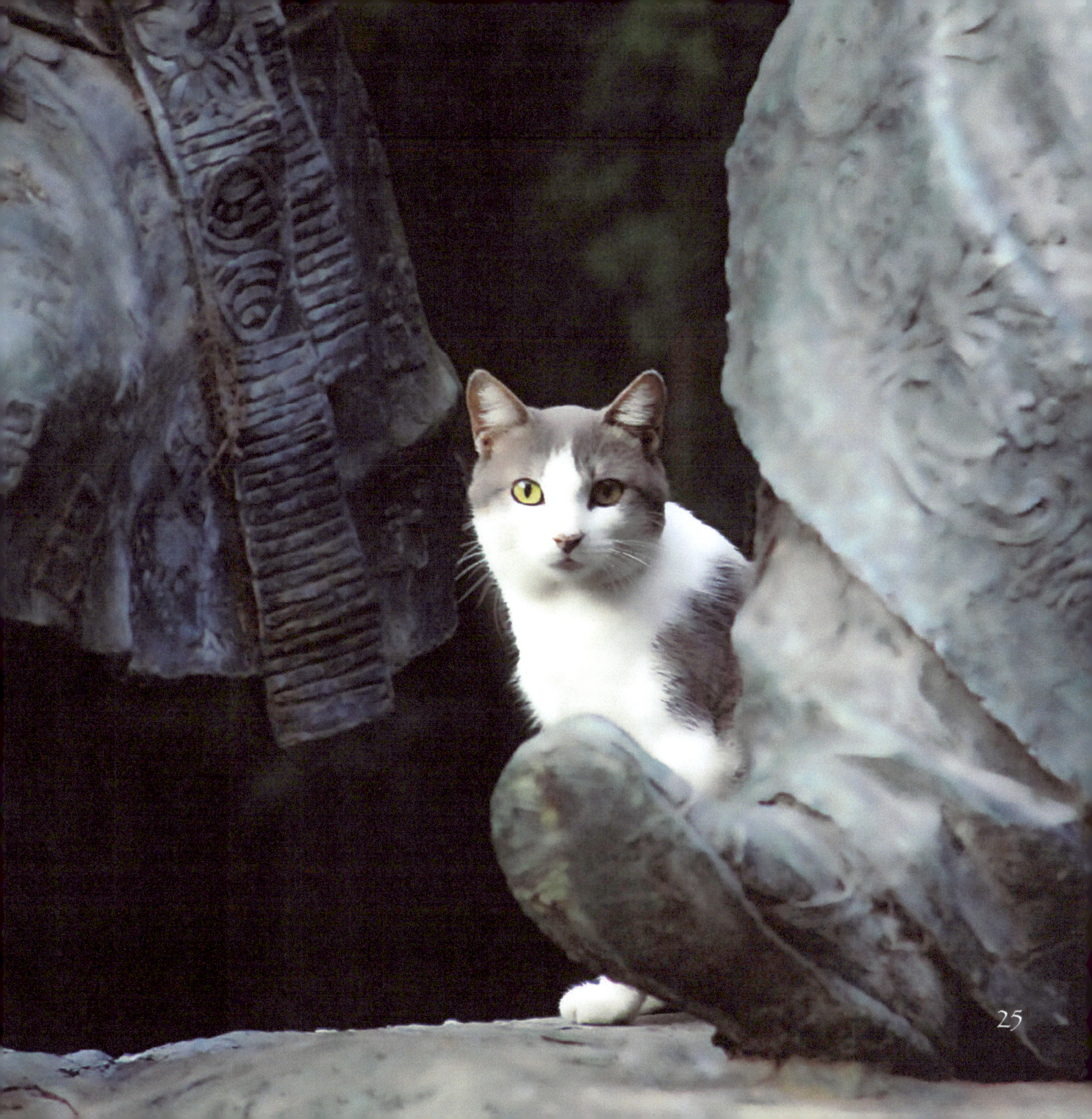

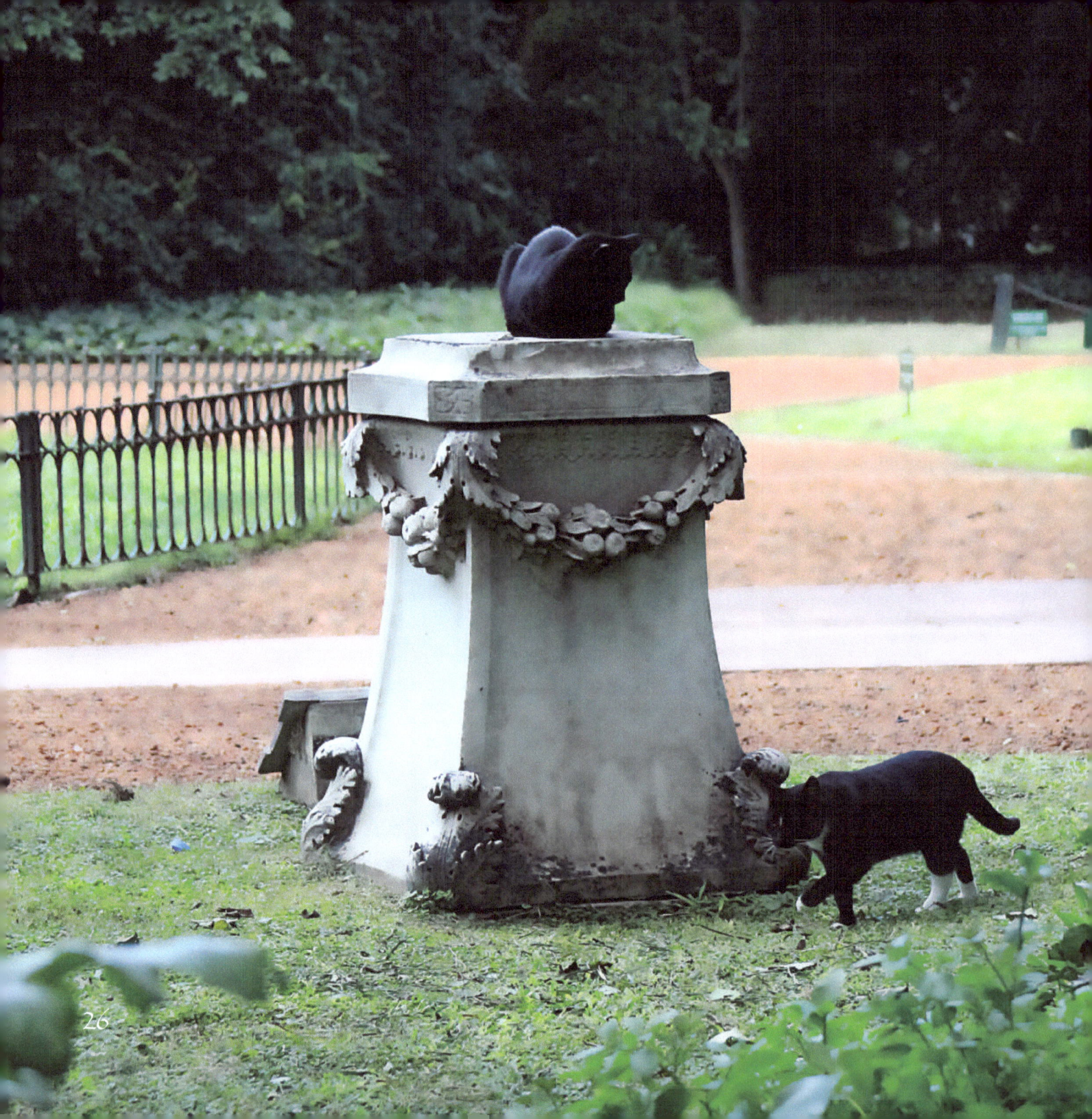

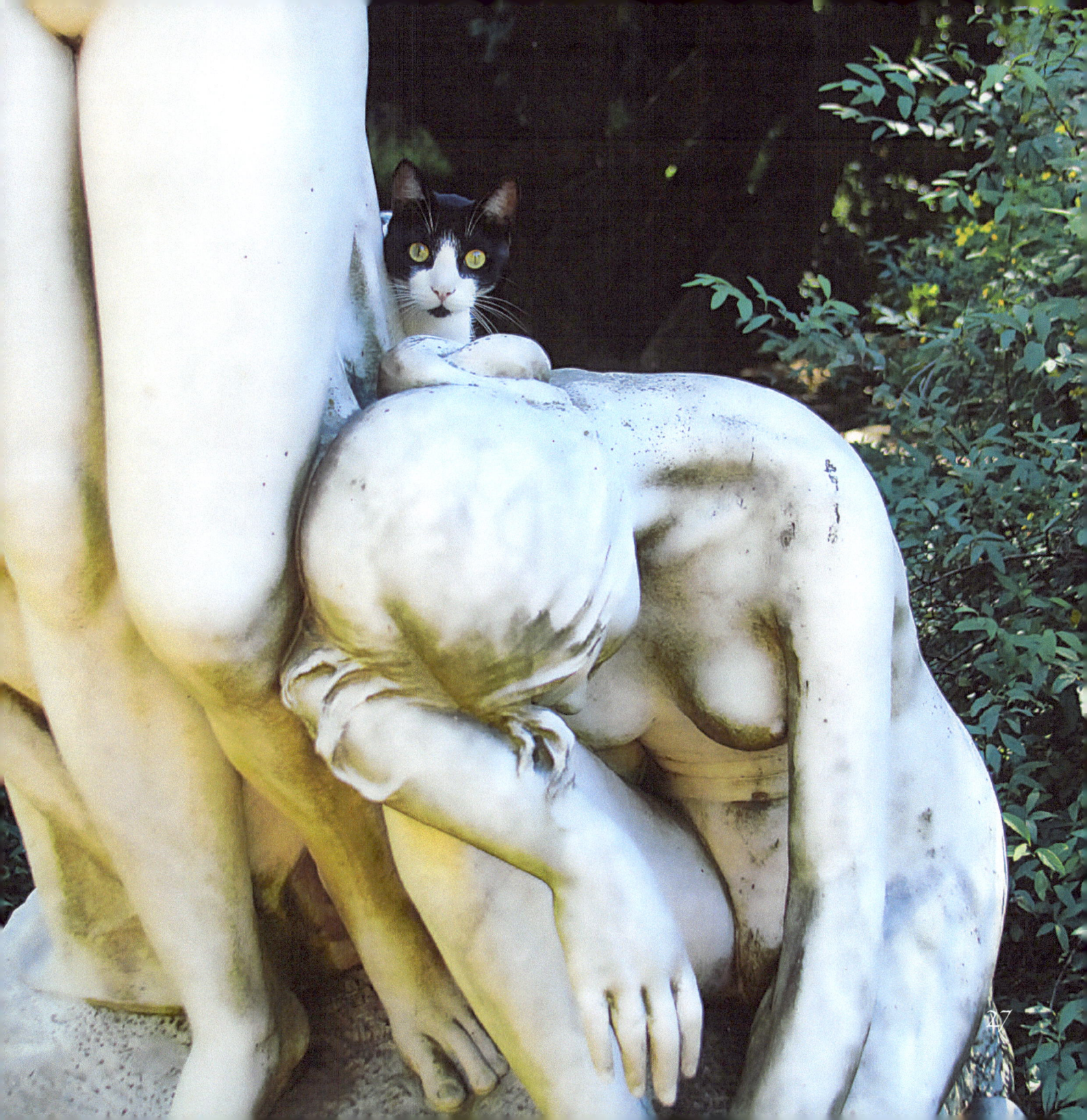

The smallest wildcat today is the Black-footed cat the females are less than 20 inches long and can weigh as little as 2.5 lbs

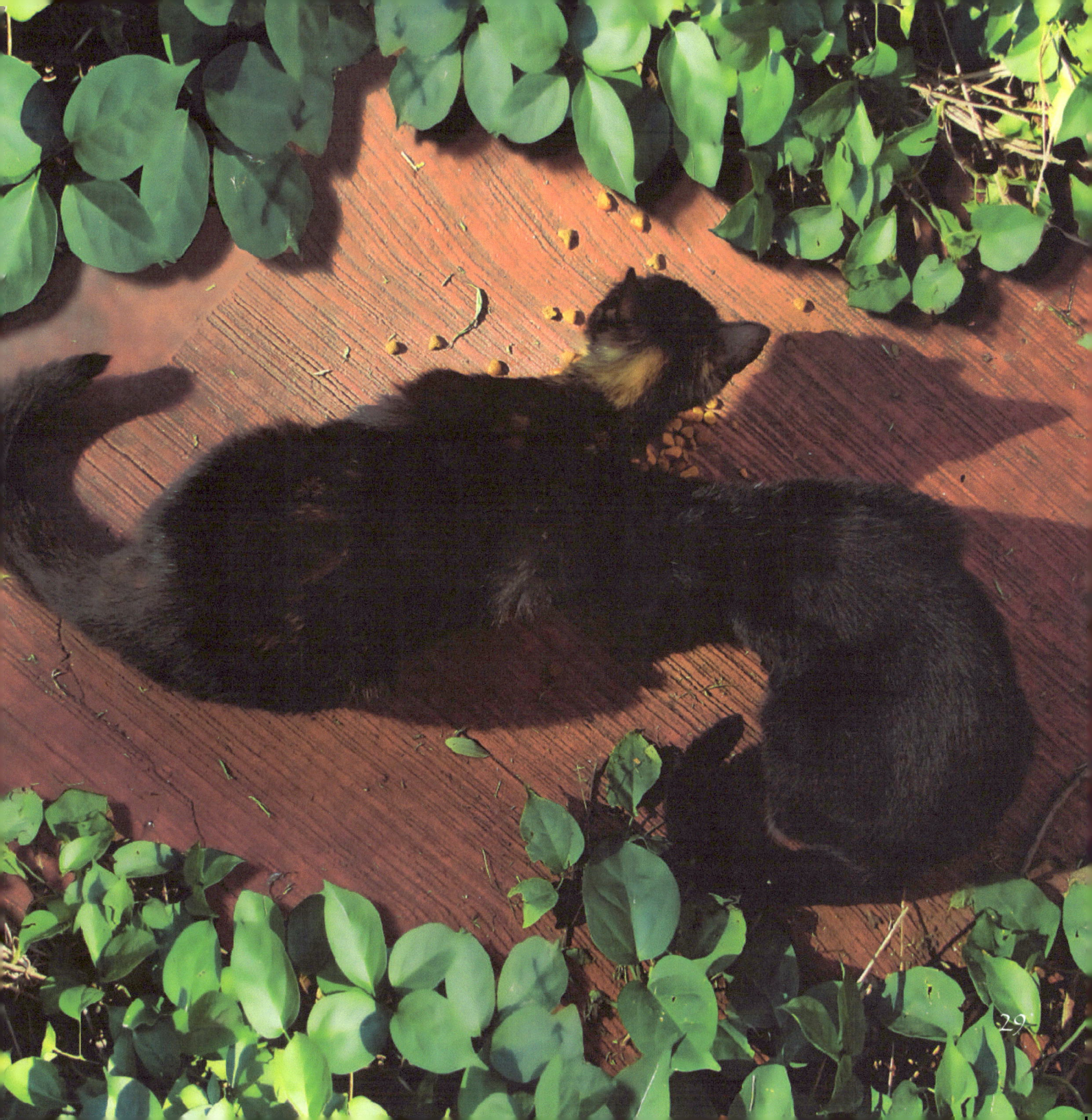

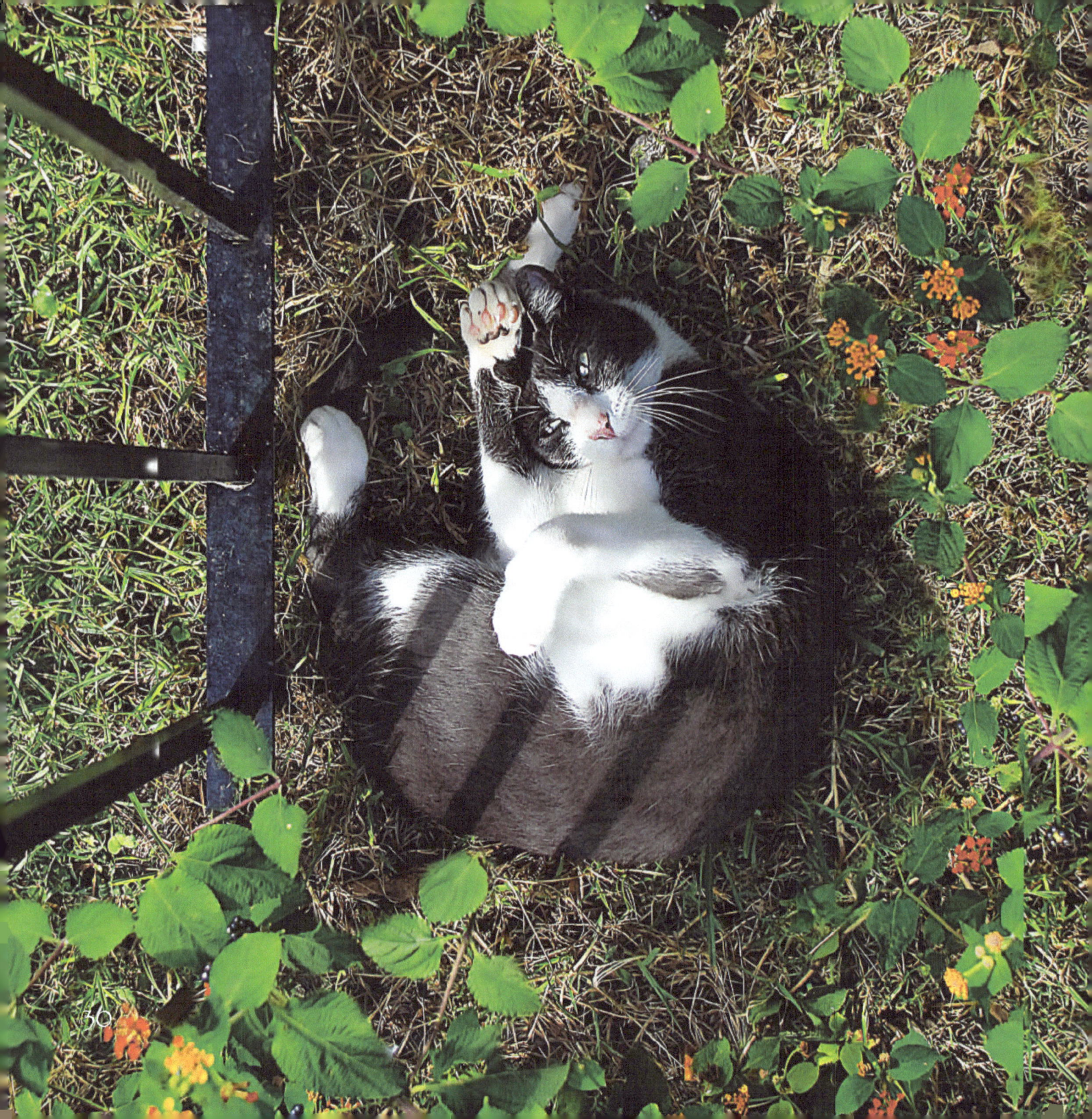

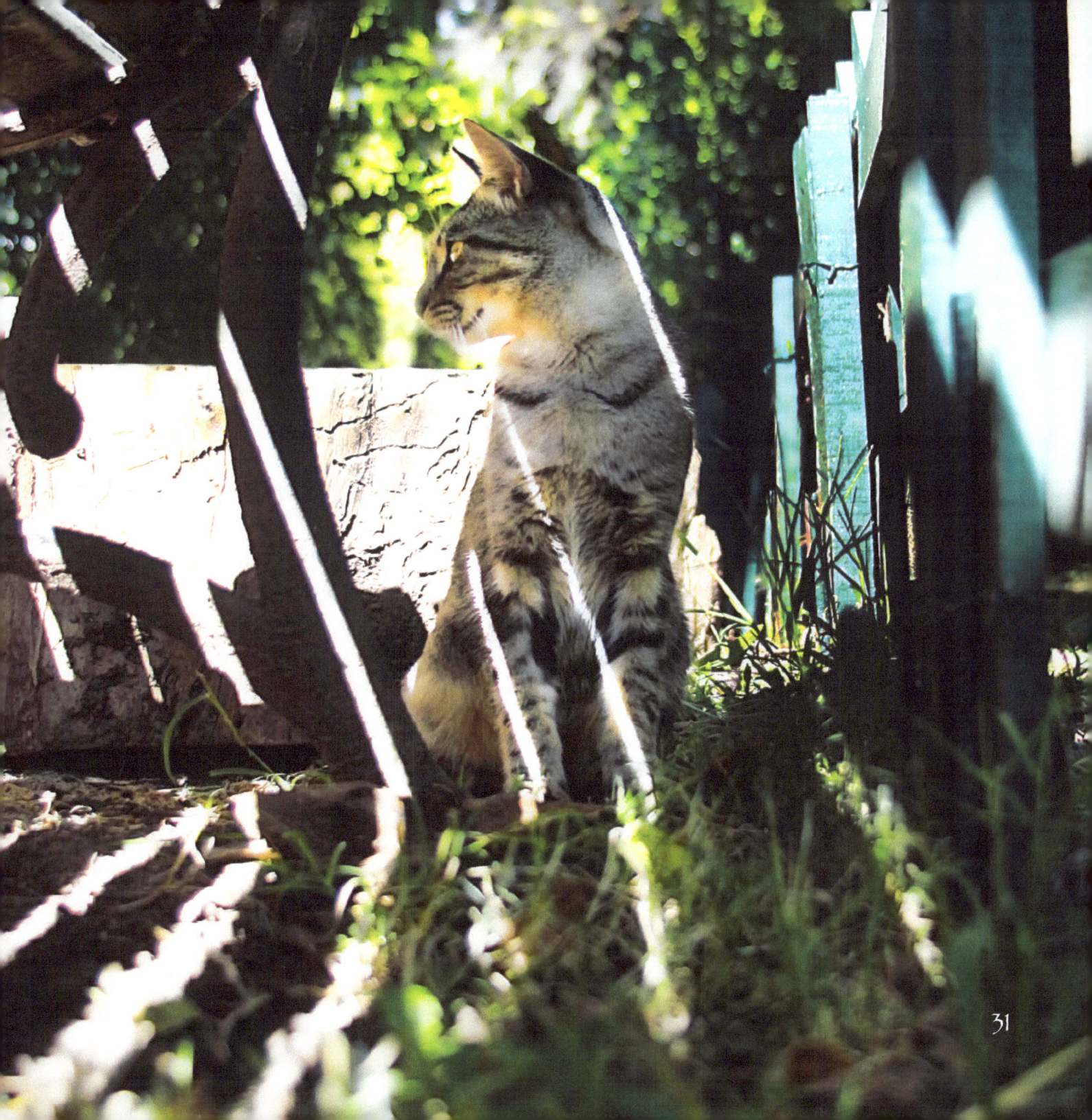

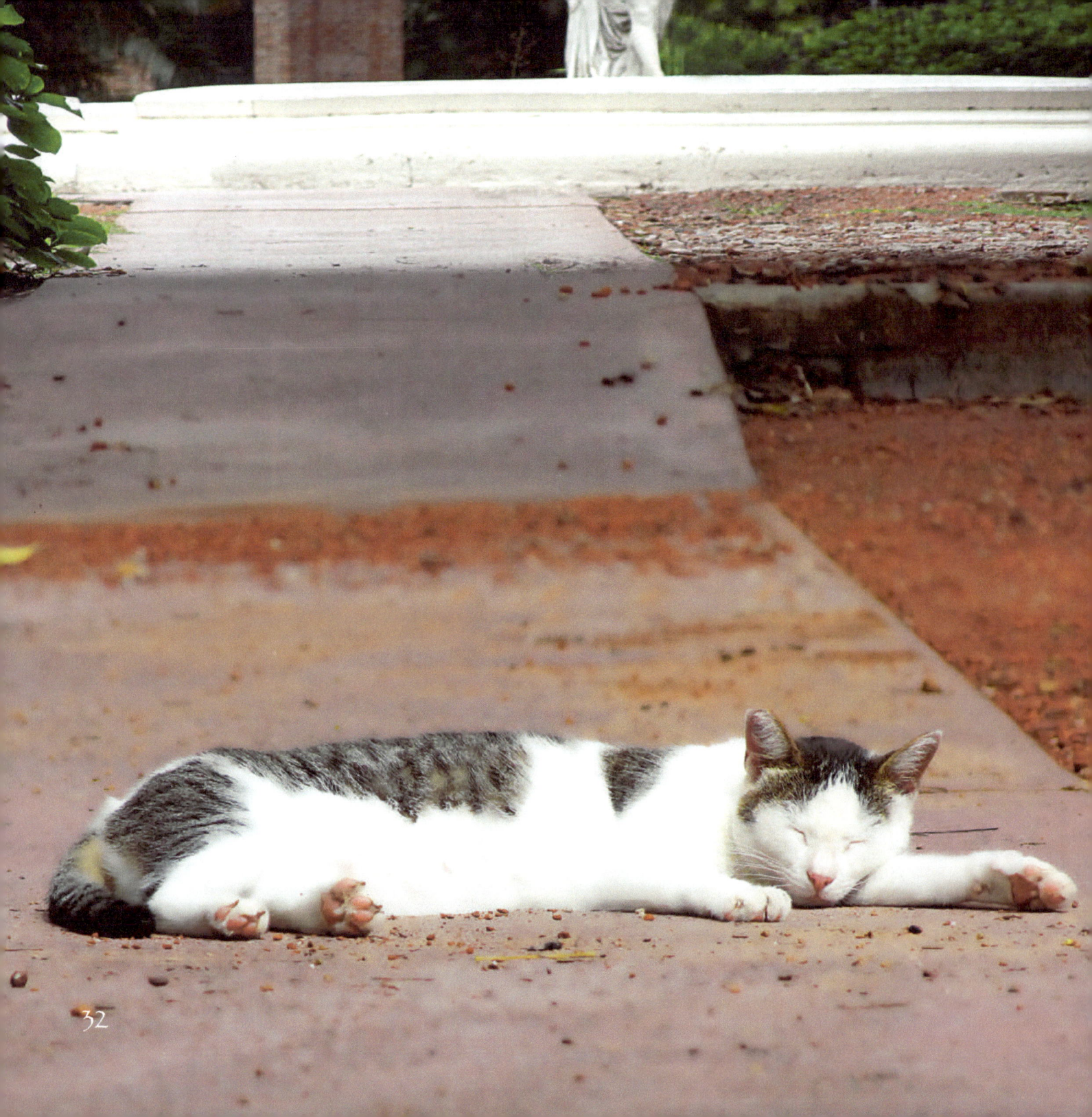

Citizens of Buenos Aires are known as Porteños

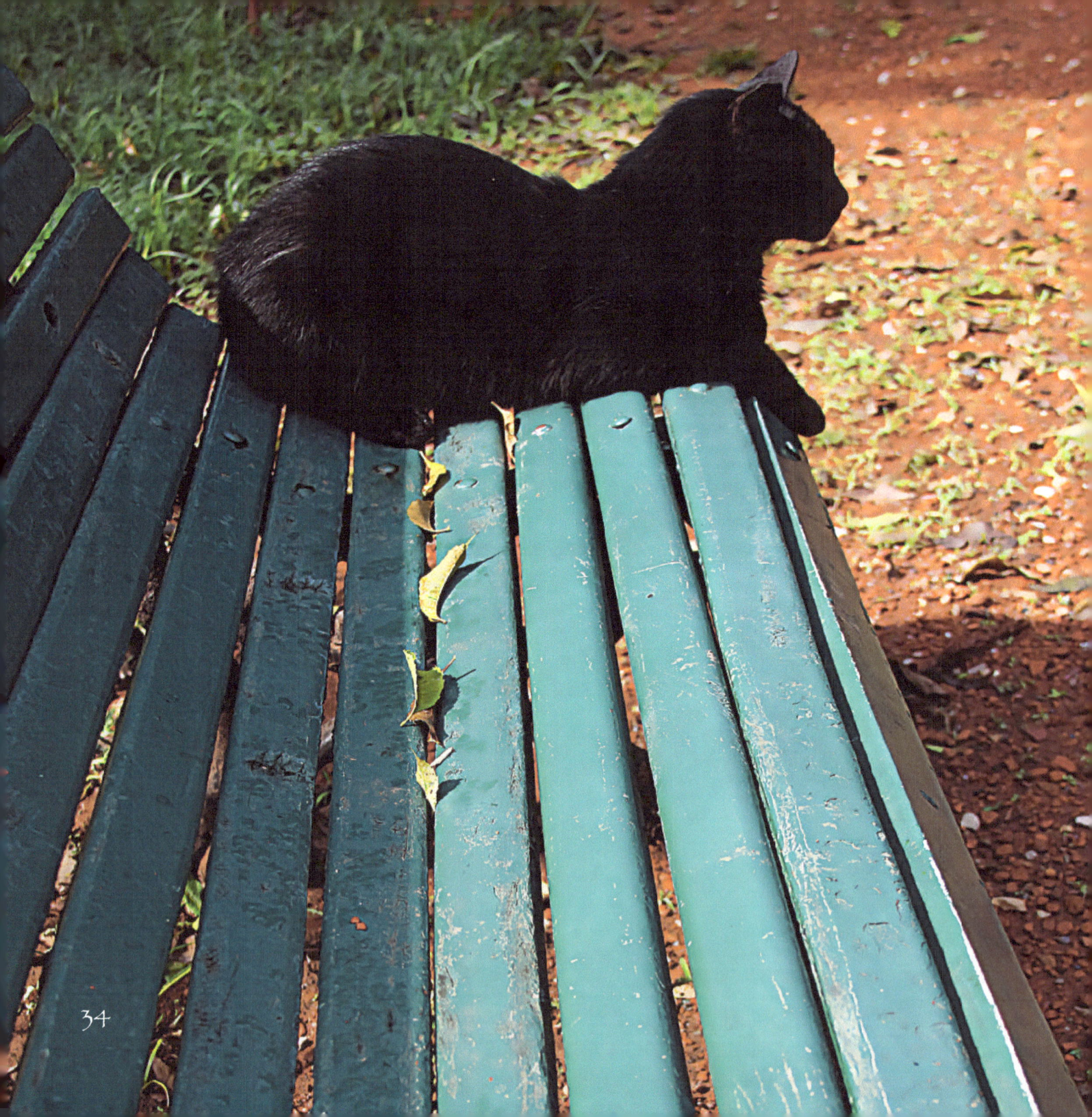

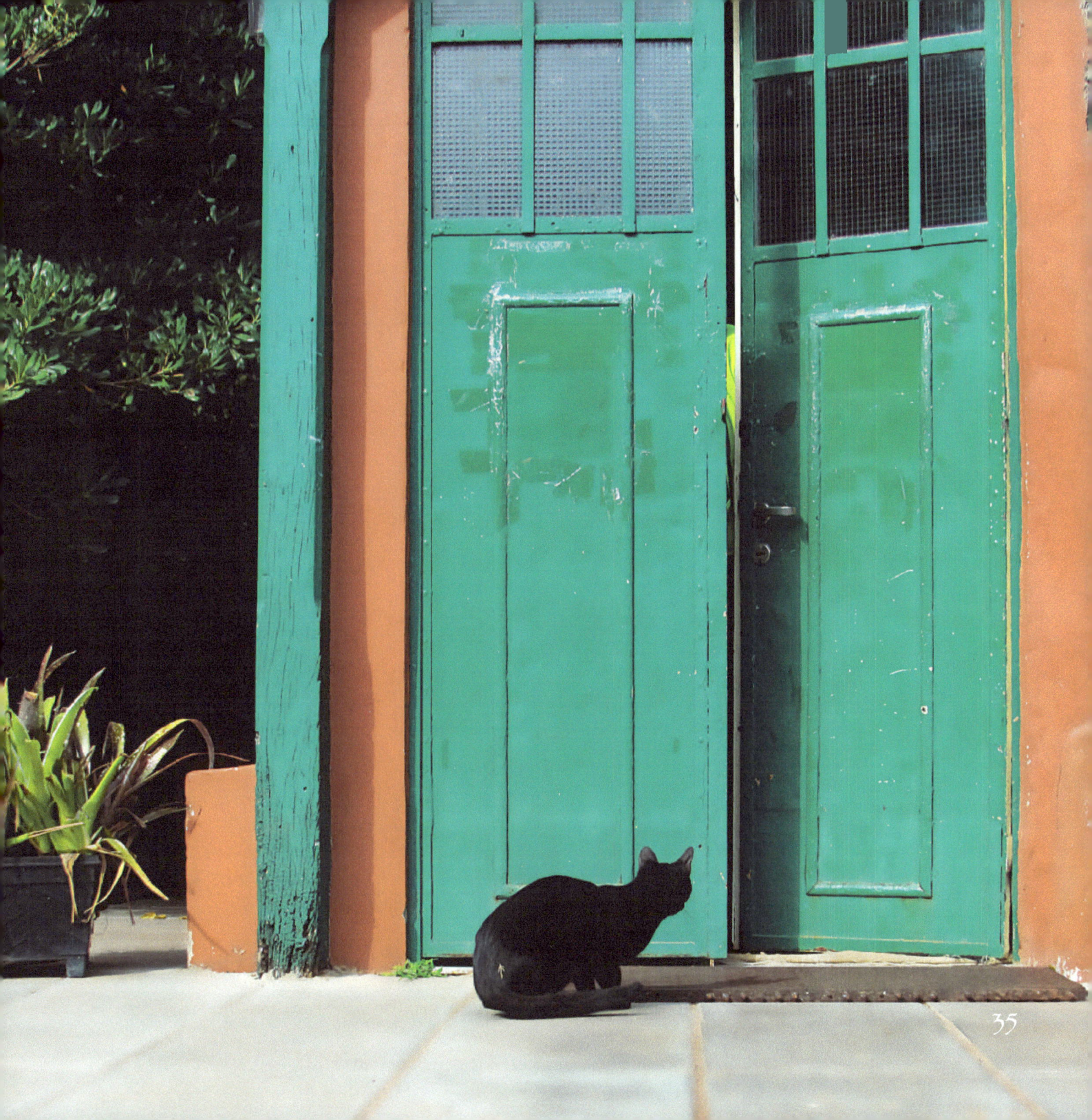

35

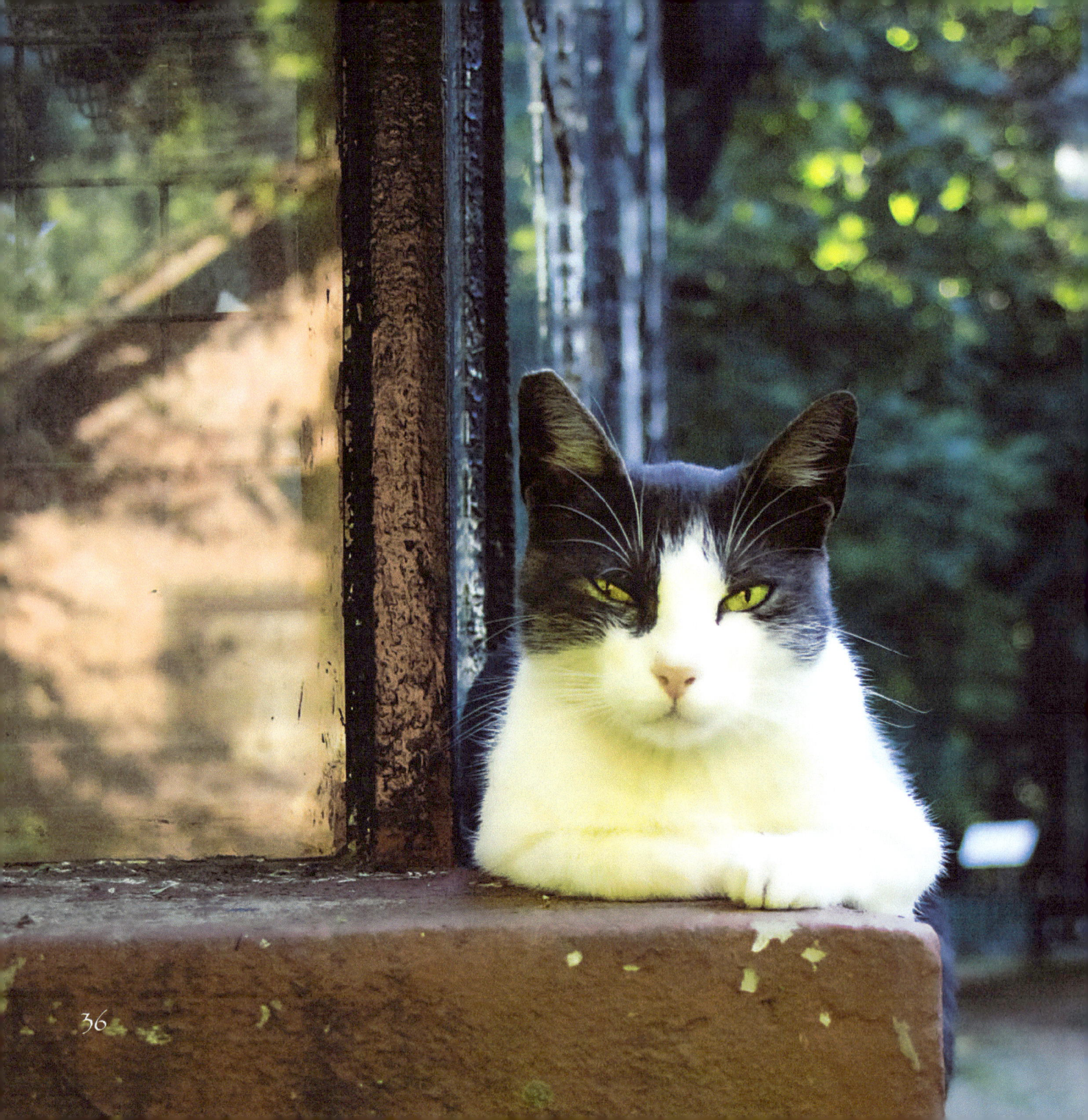

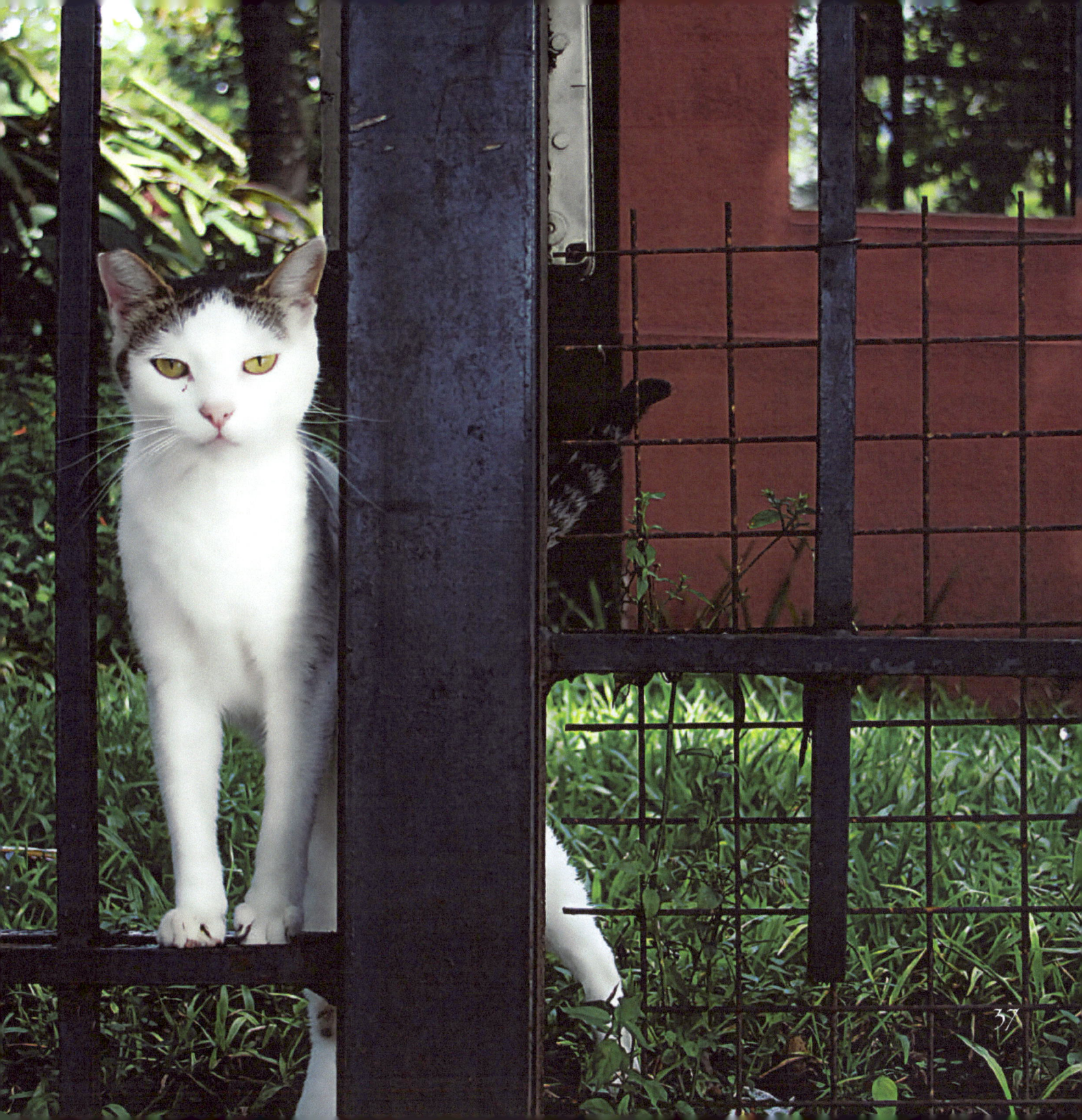

A cat's jaw can only move up and down, it does not have any lateral or side to side motion

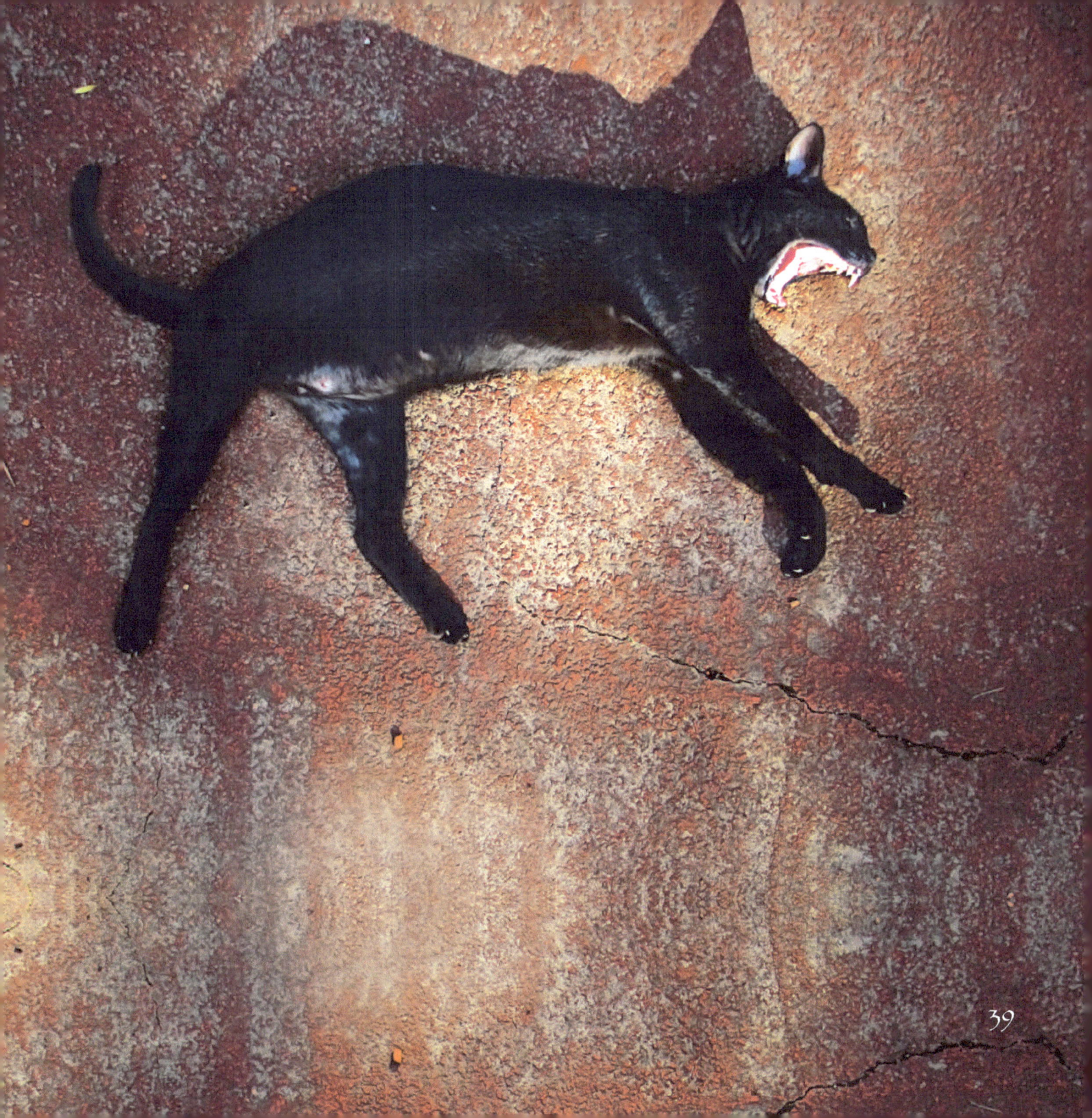

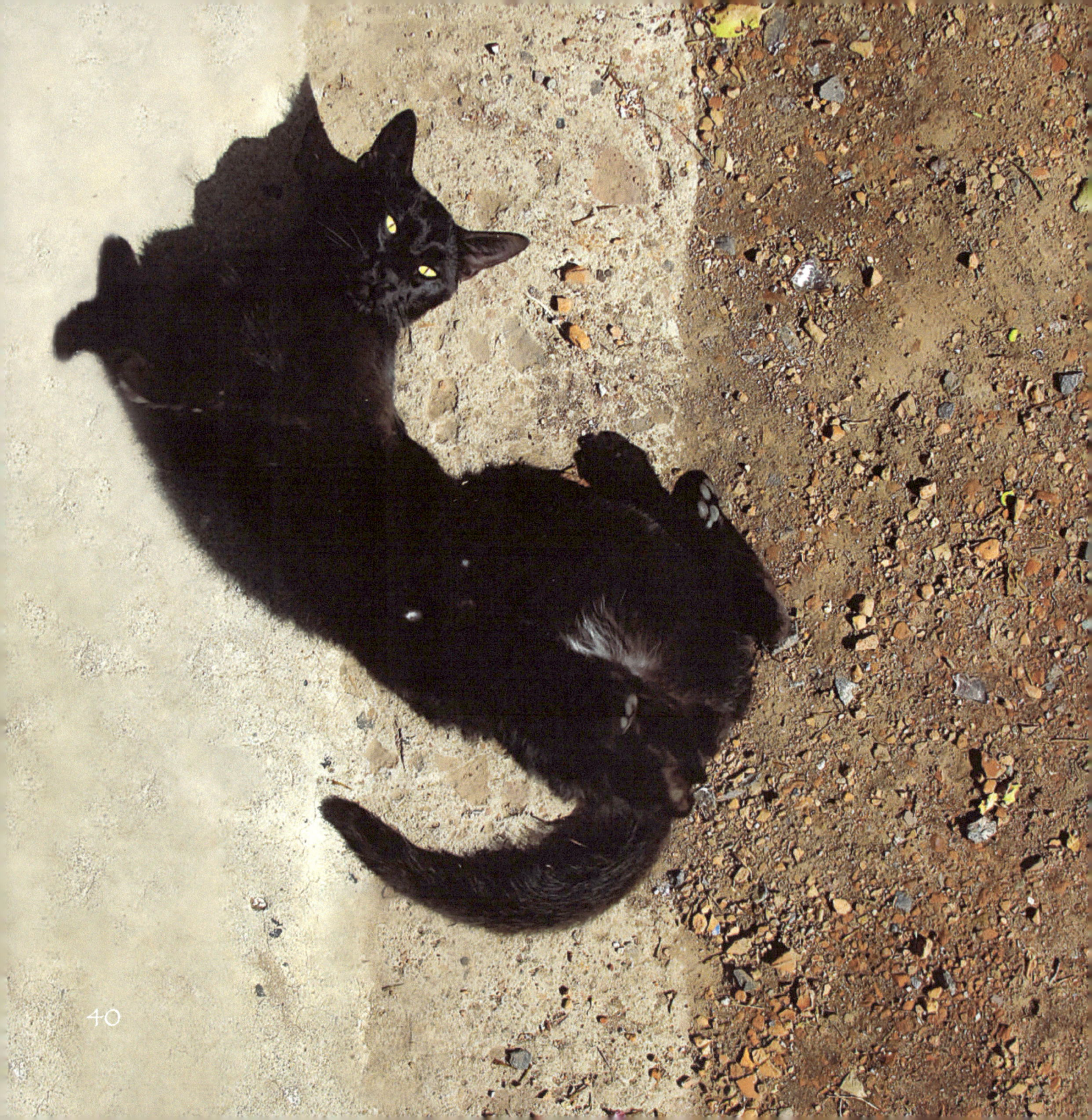

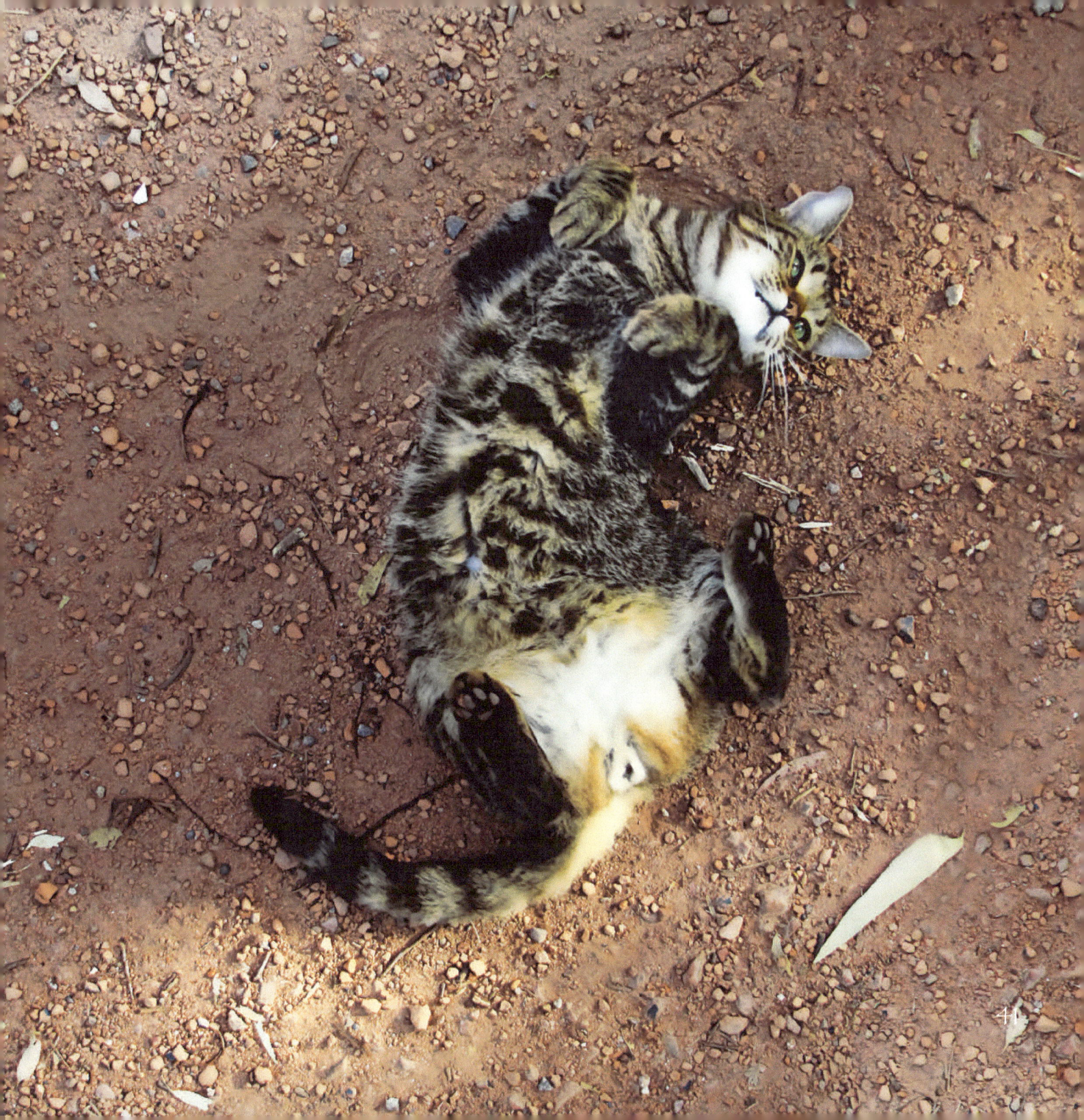

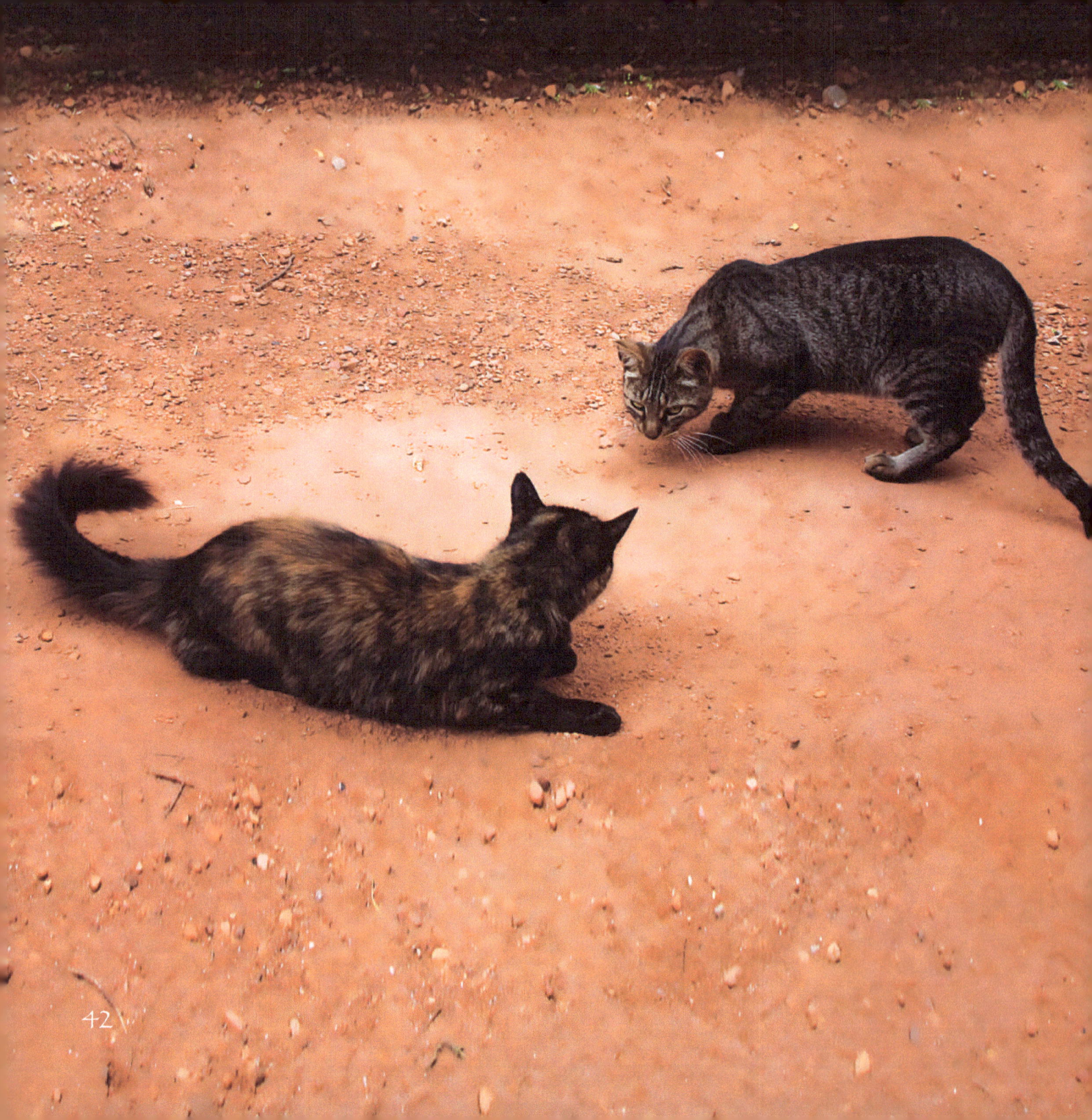

The President's Mansion in Buenos Aires is called Casa Rosada or Pink House

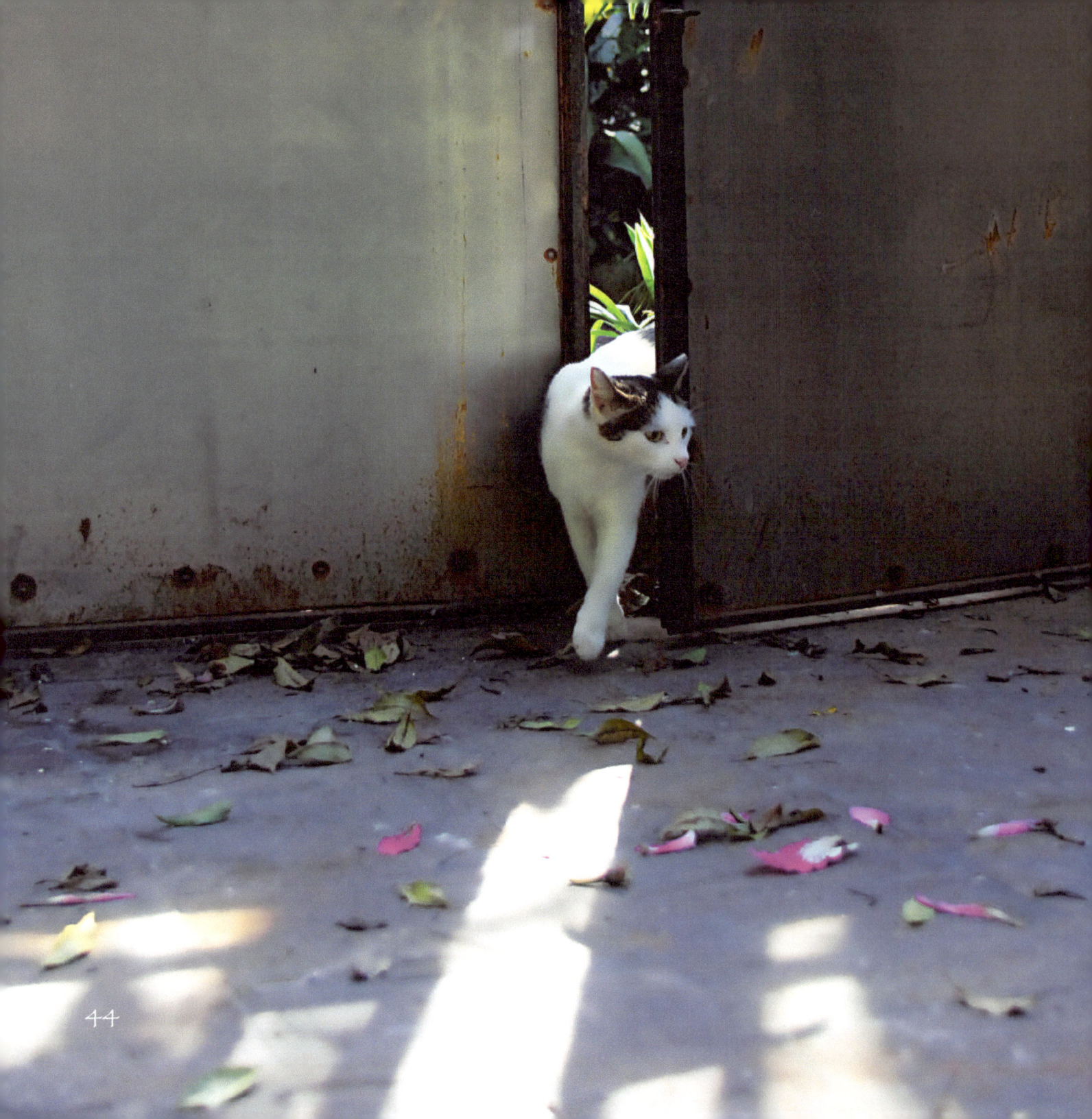

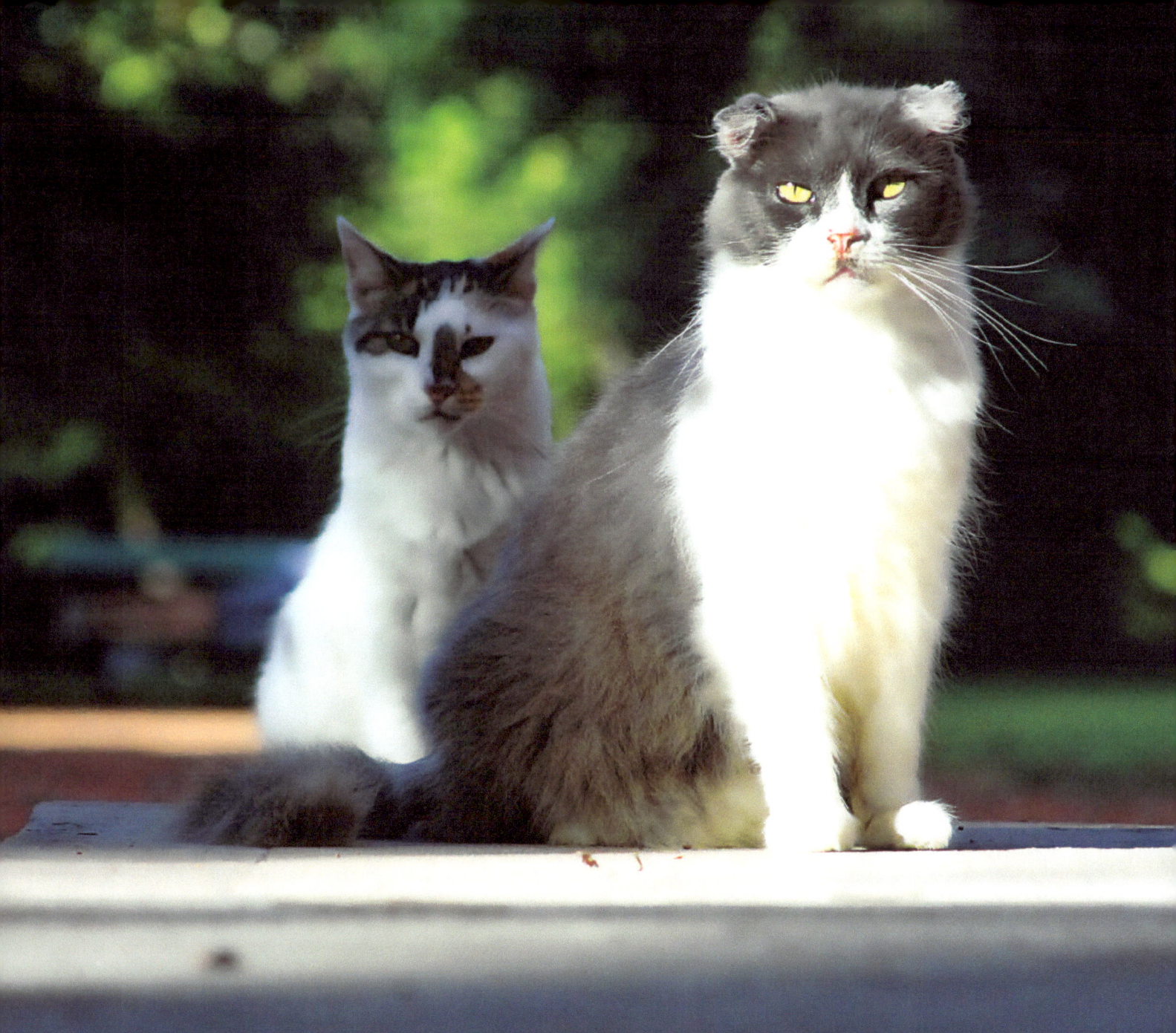

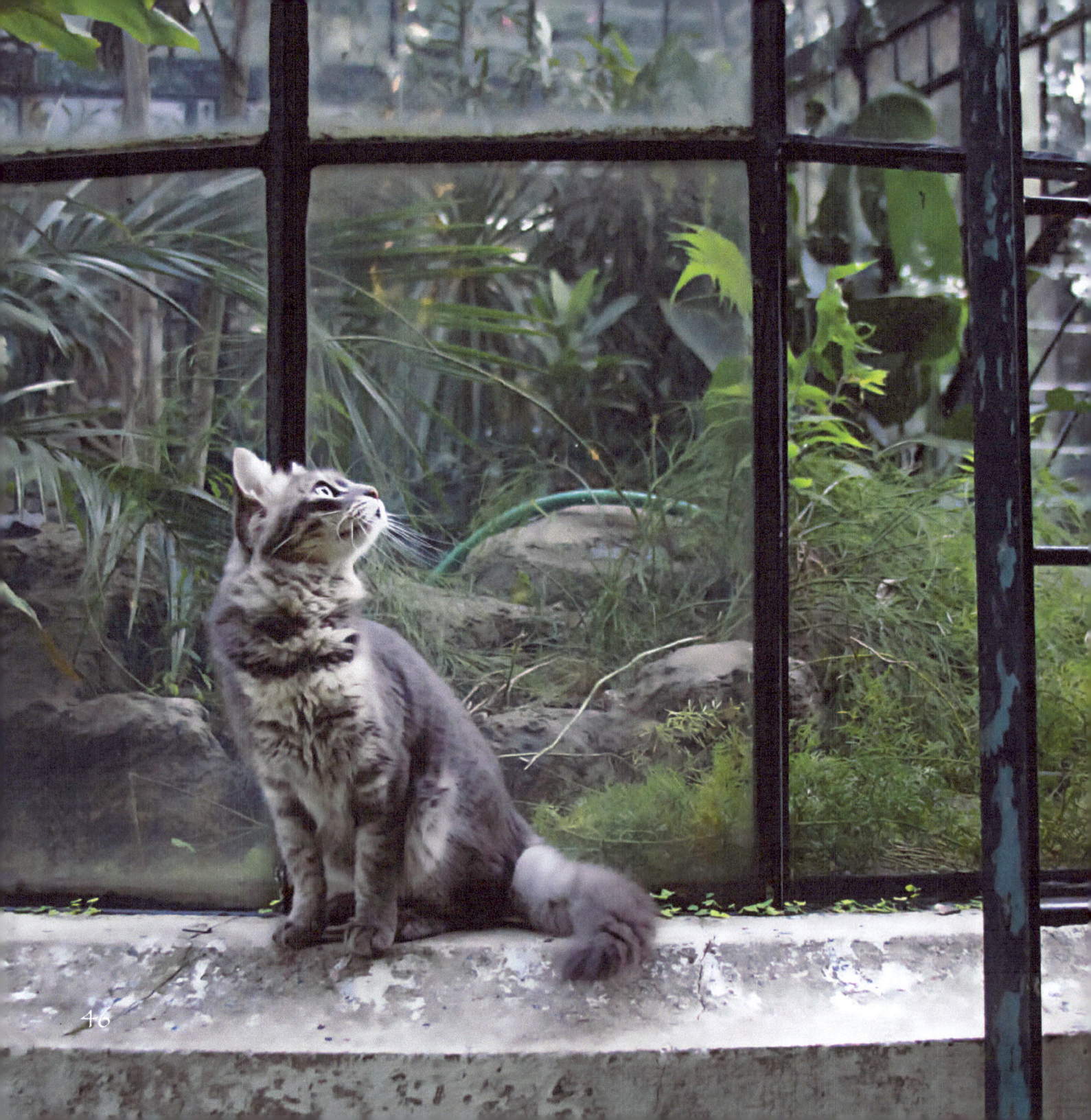

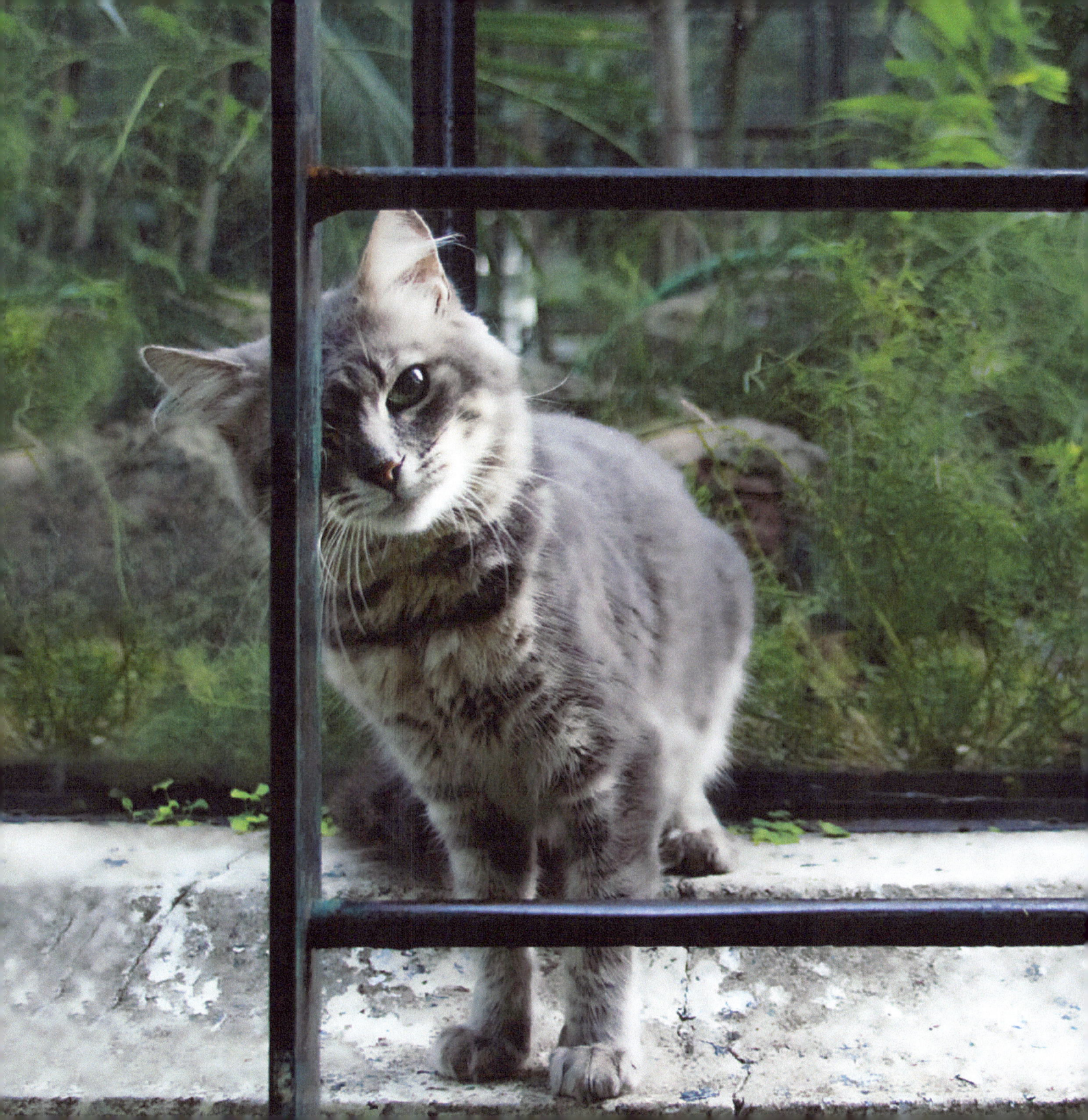

The domestic cat is the only species able to hold its tail vertically while walking

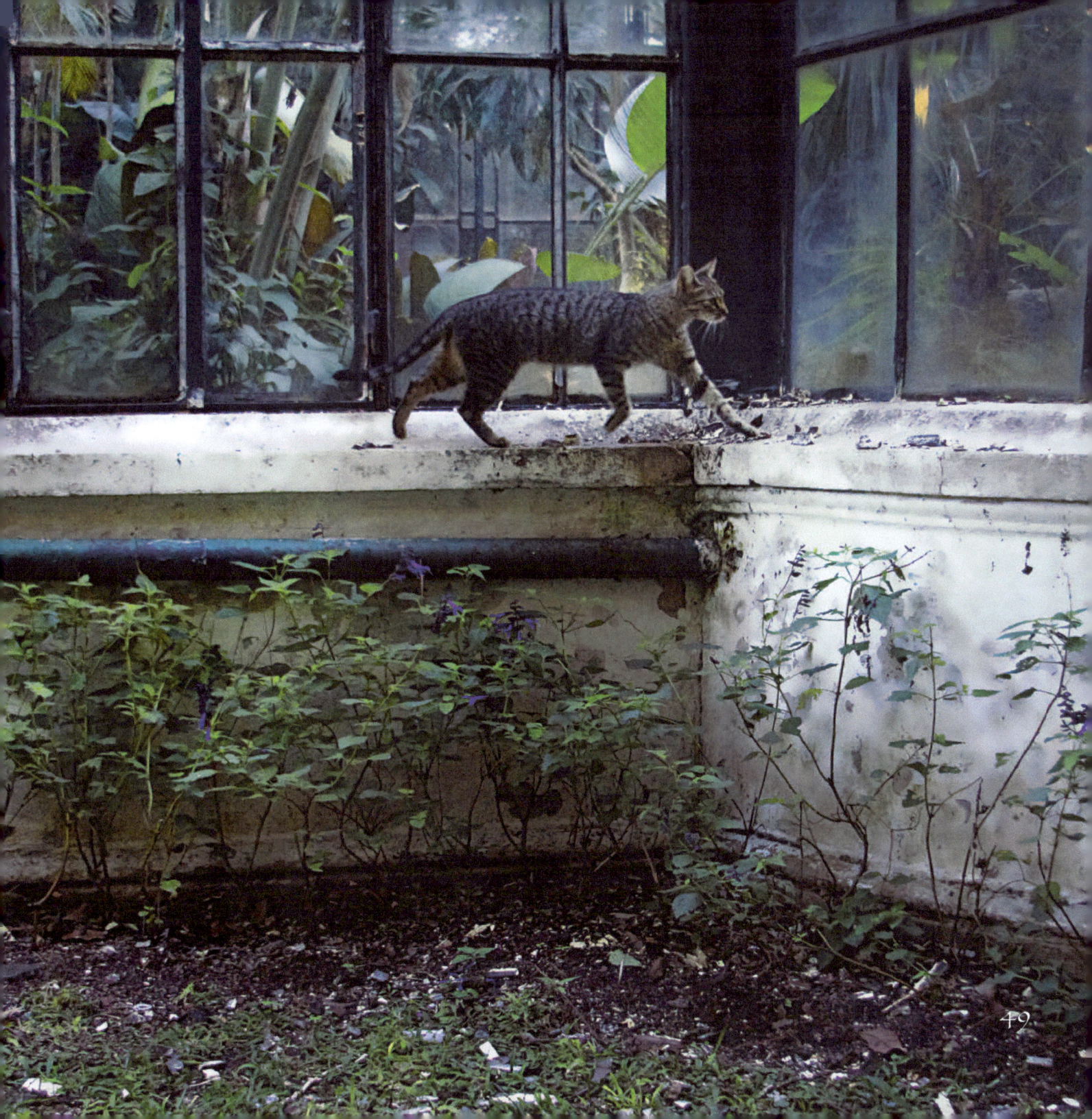

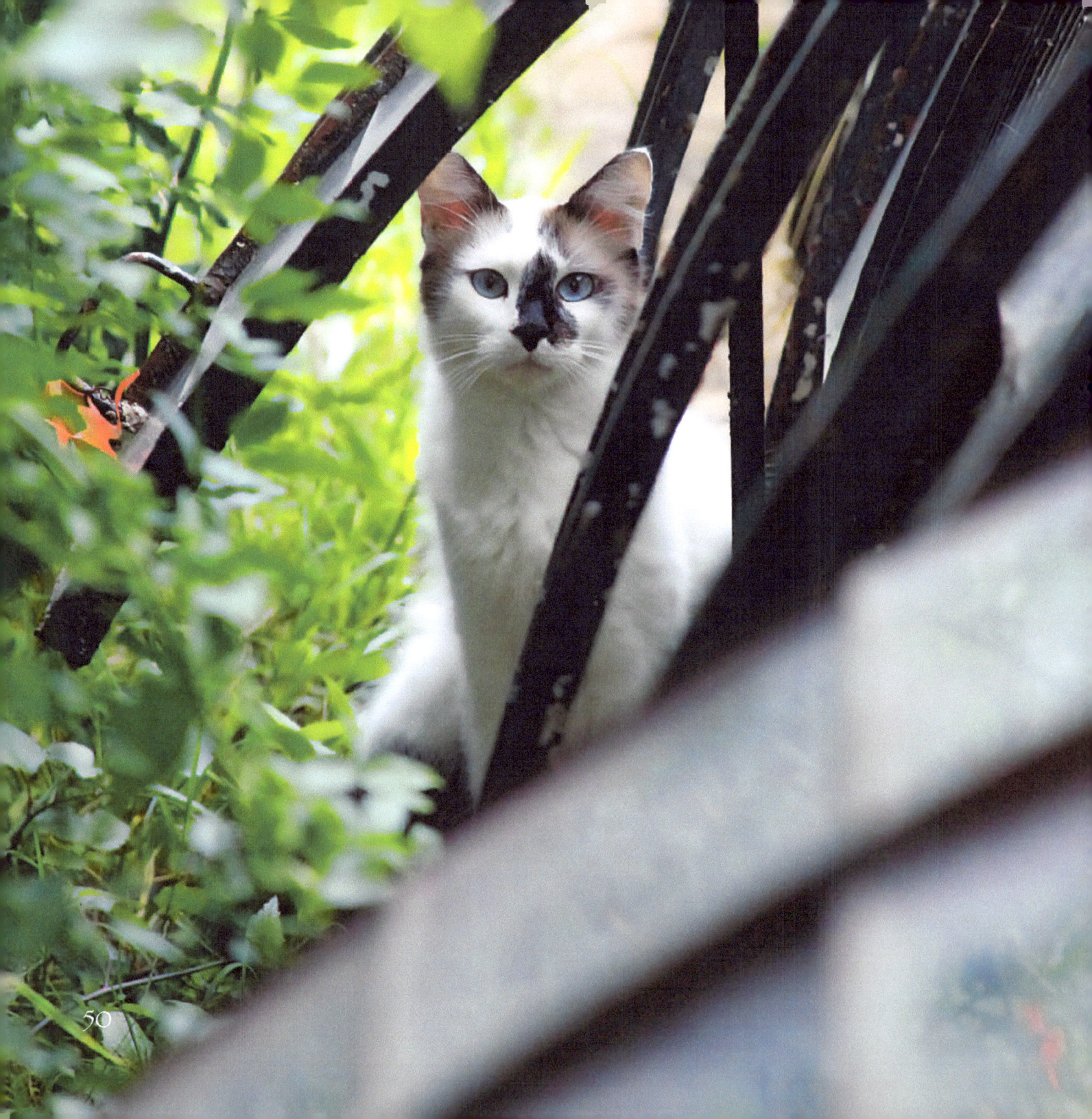

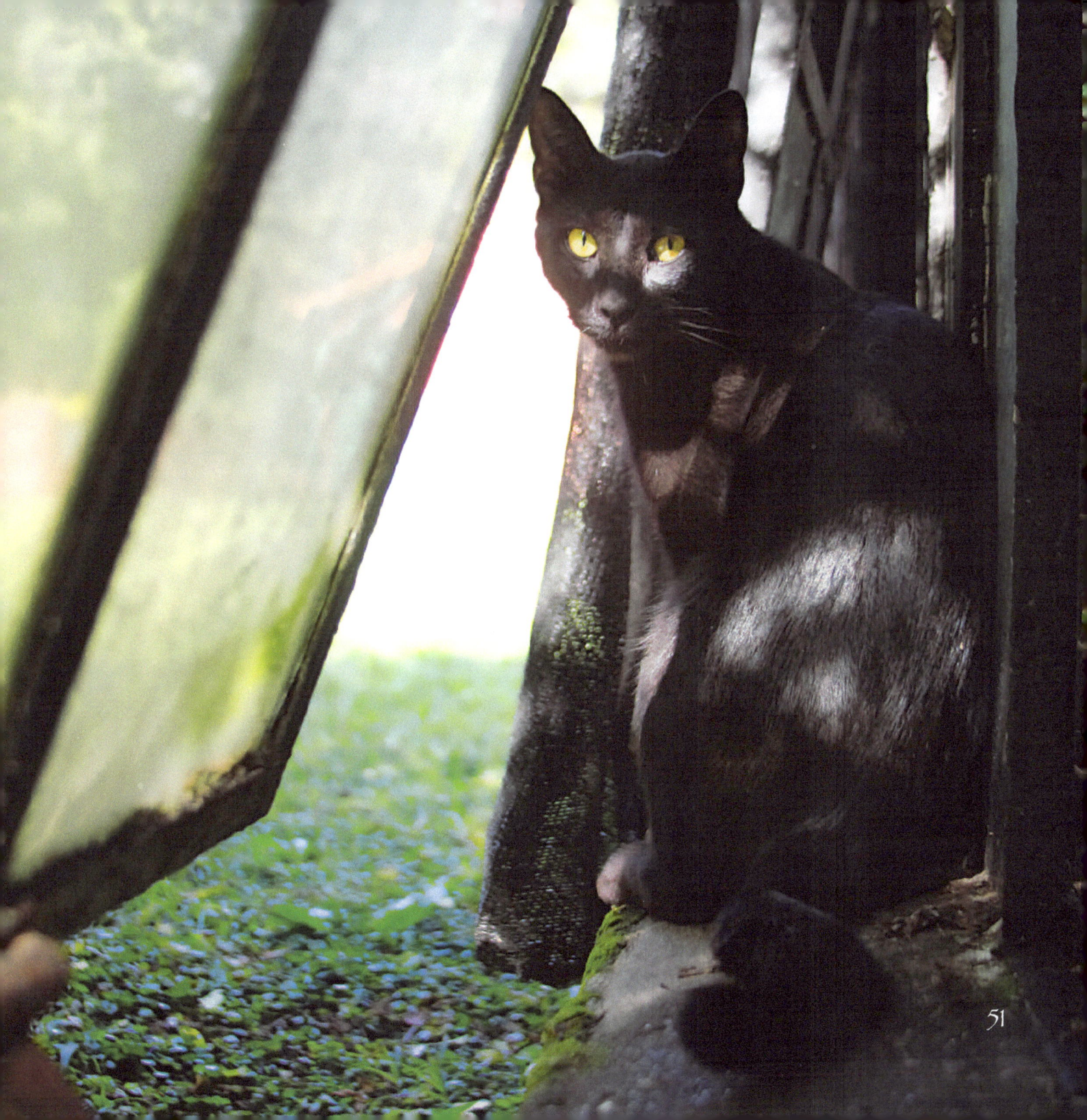

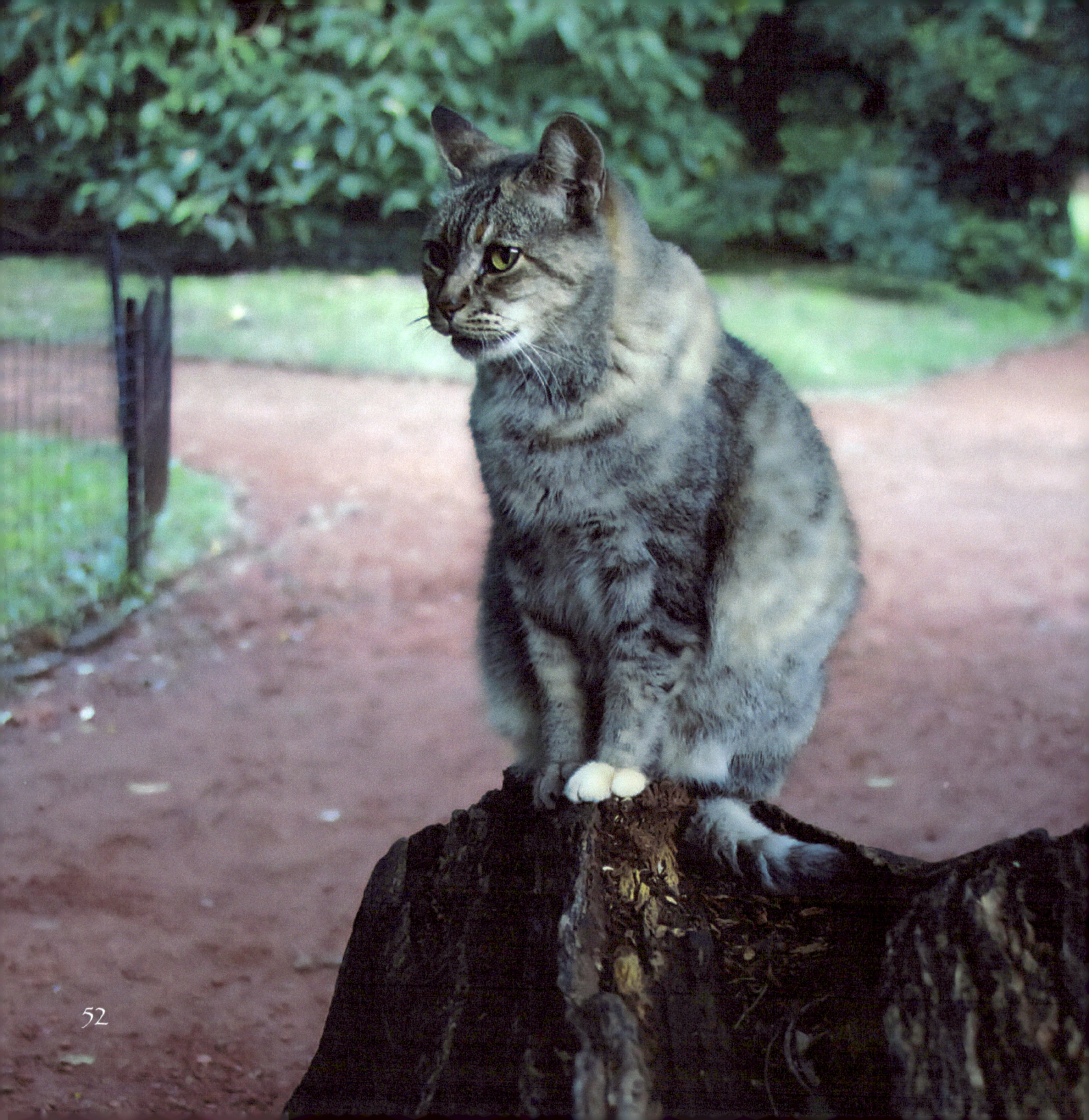

52

Buenos Aires has the most bookstores per person of any city in the world with one location for every 4000 citizens

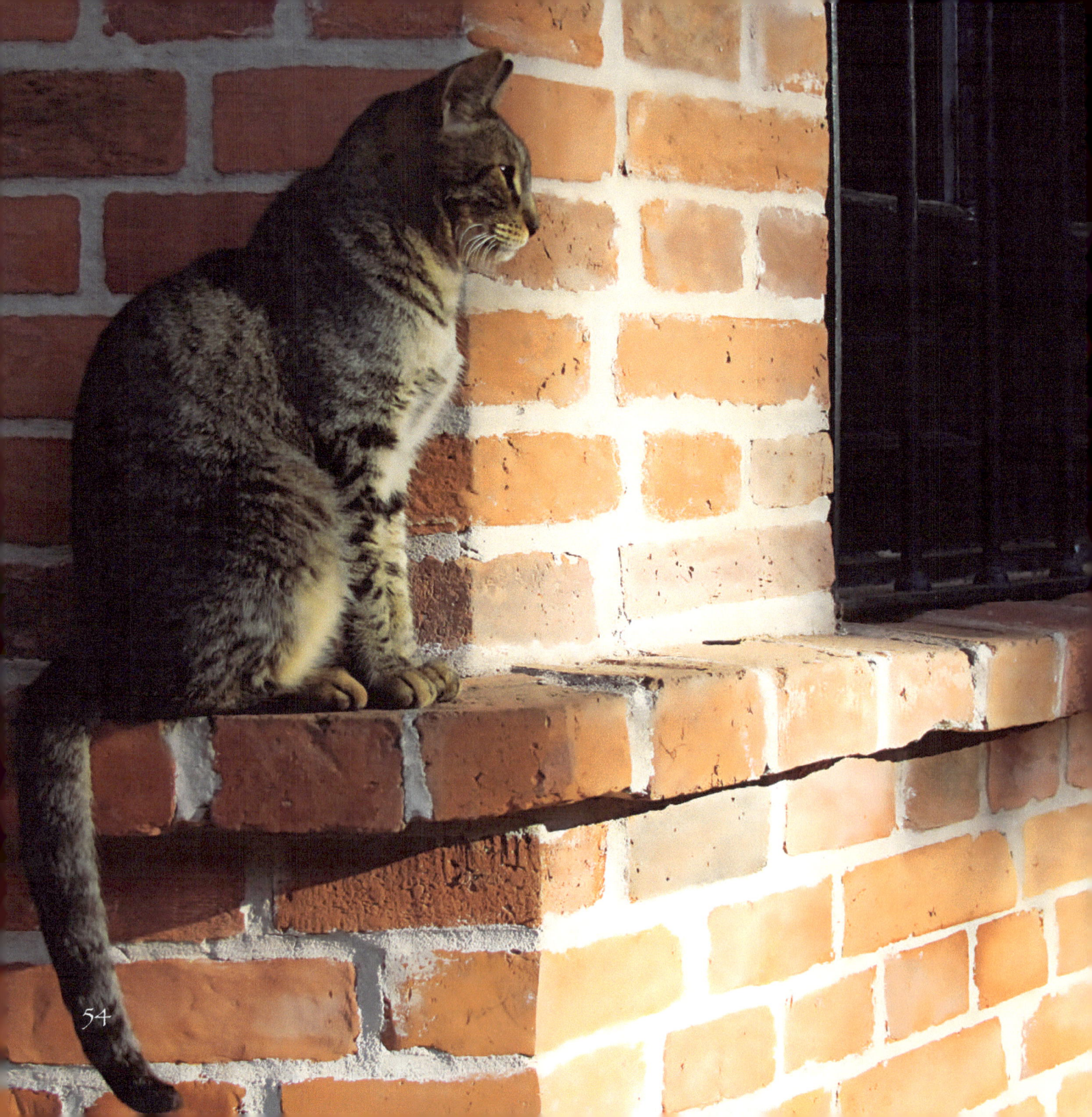

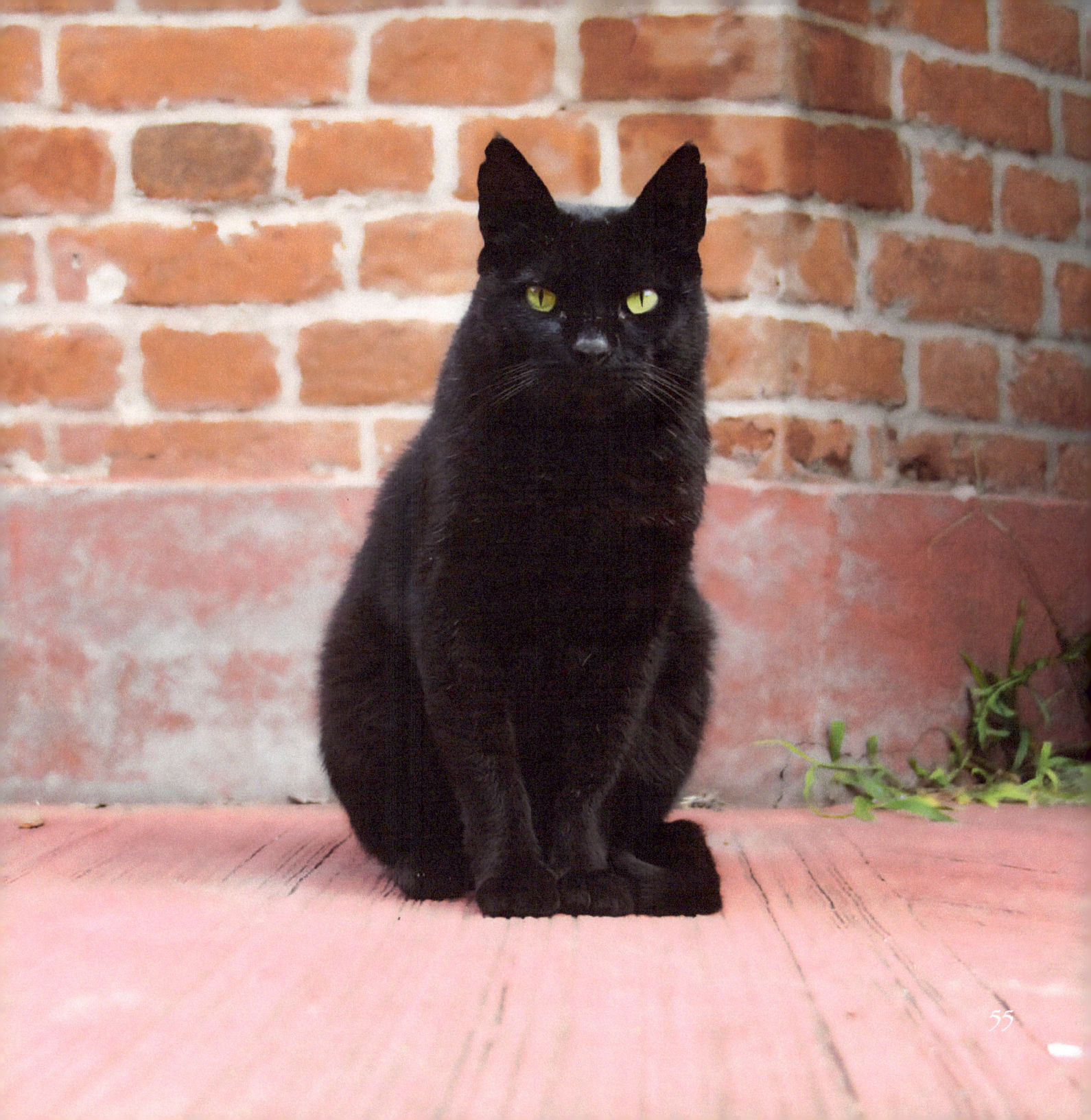

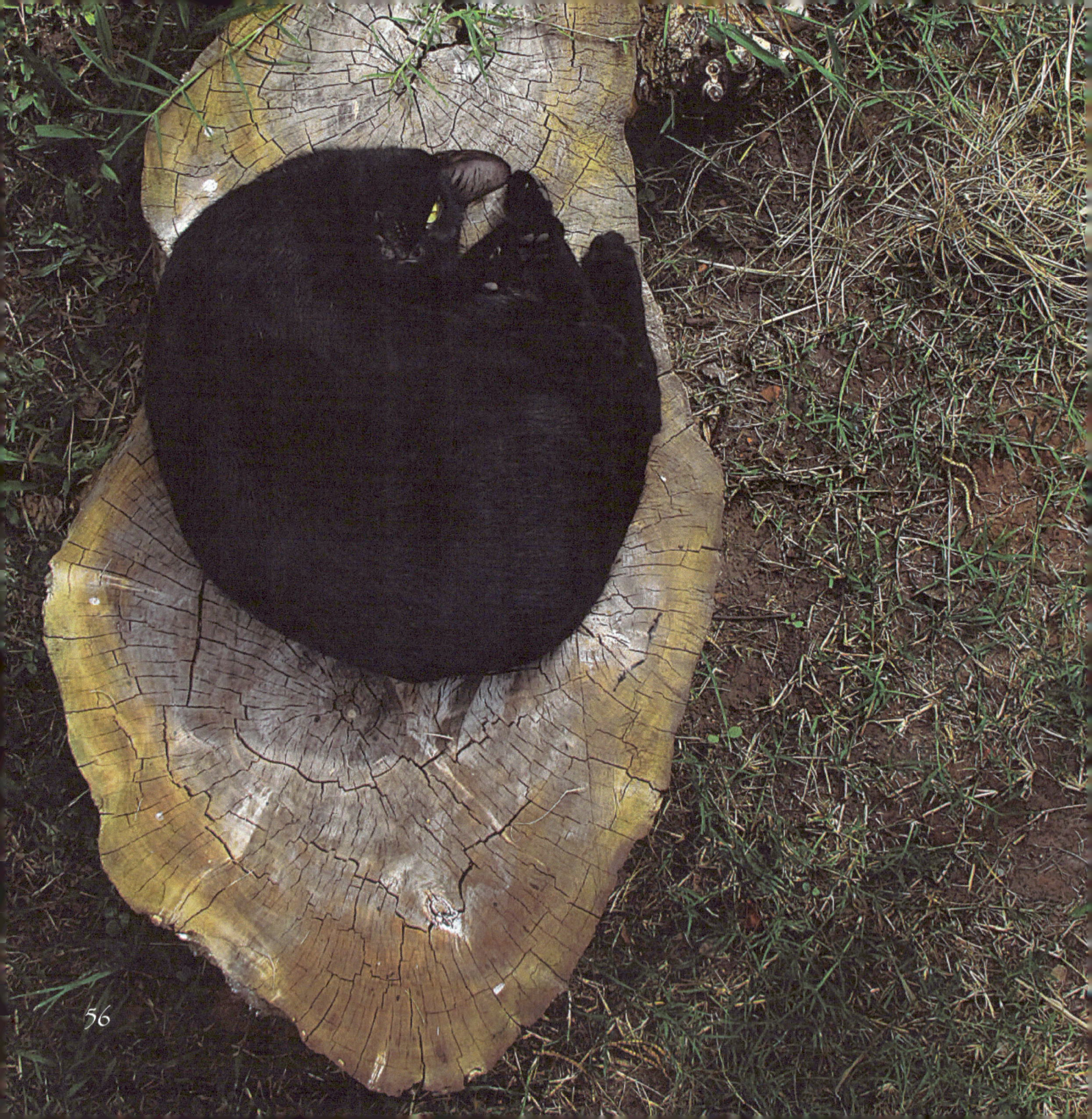

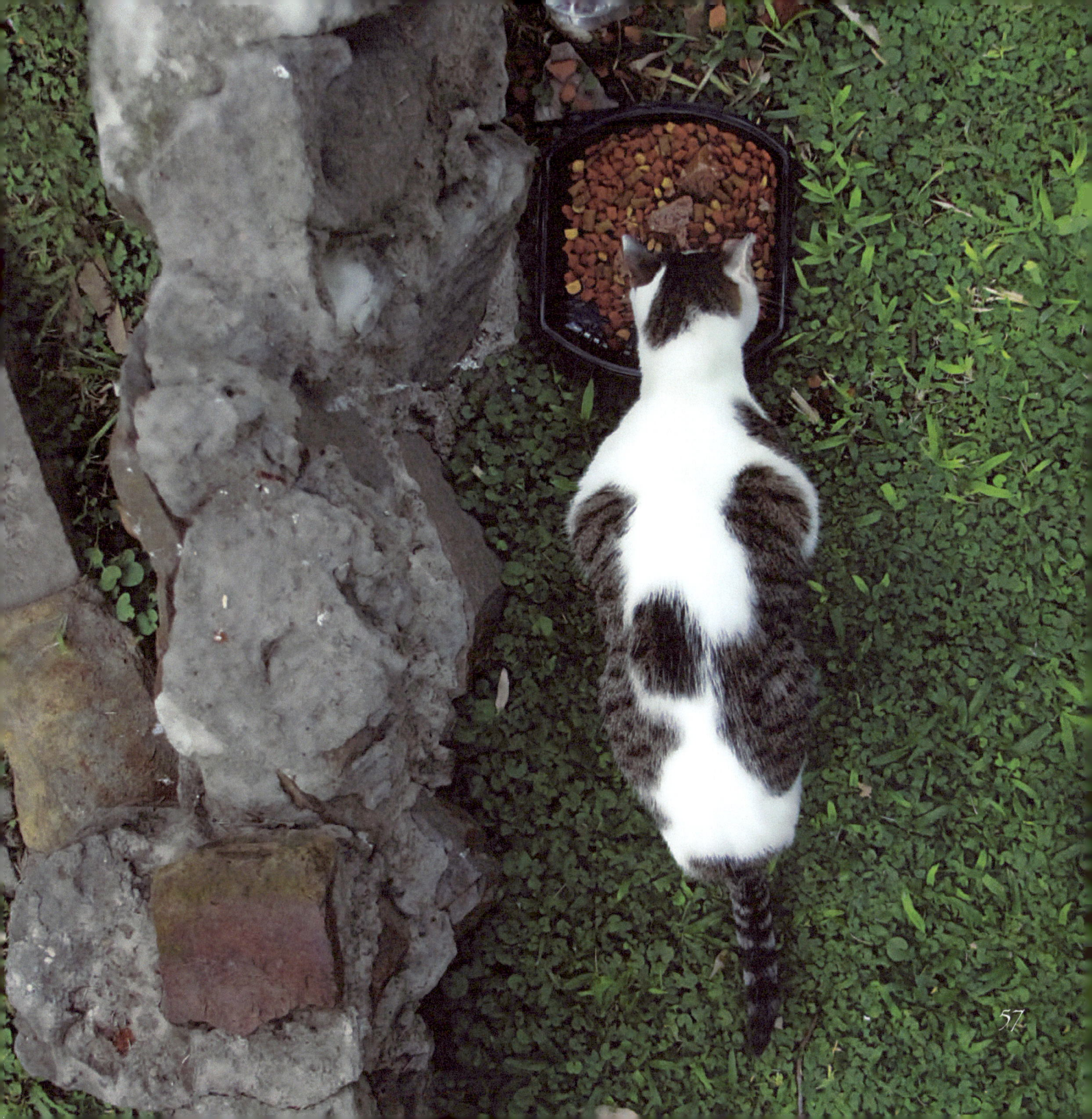

A Calico cat is usually female

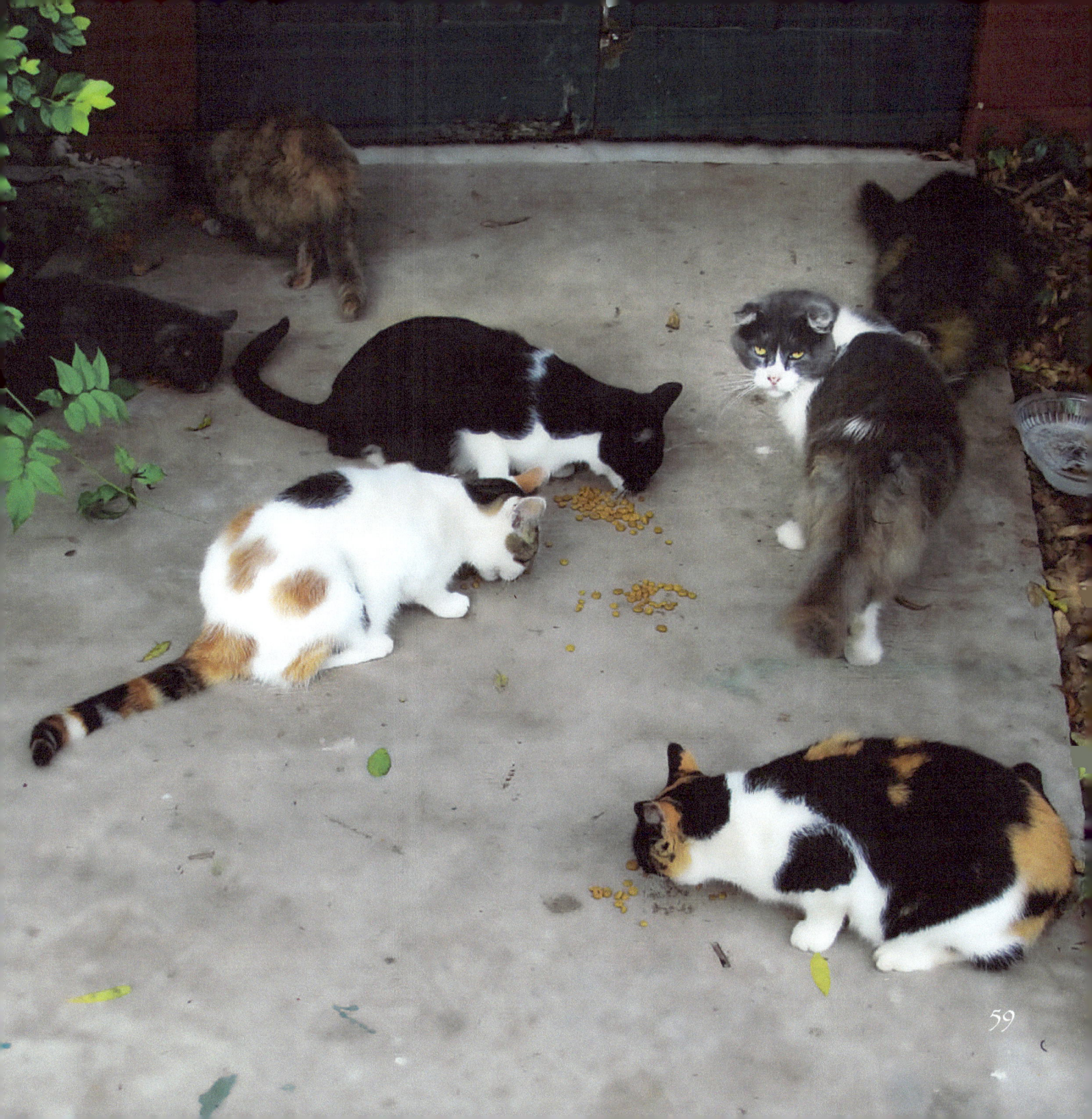

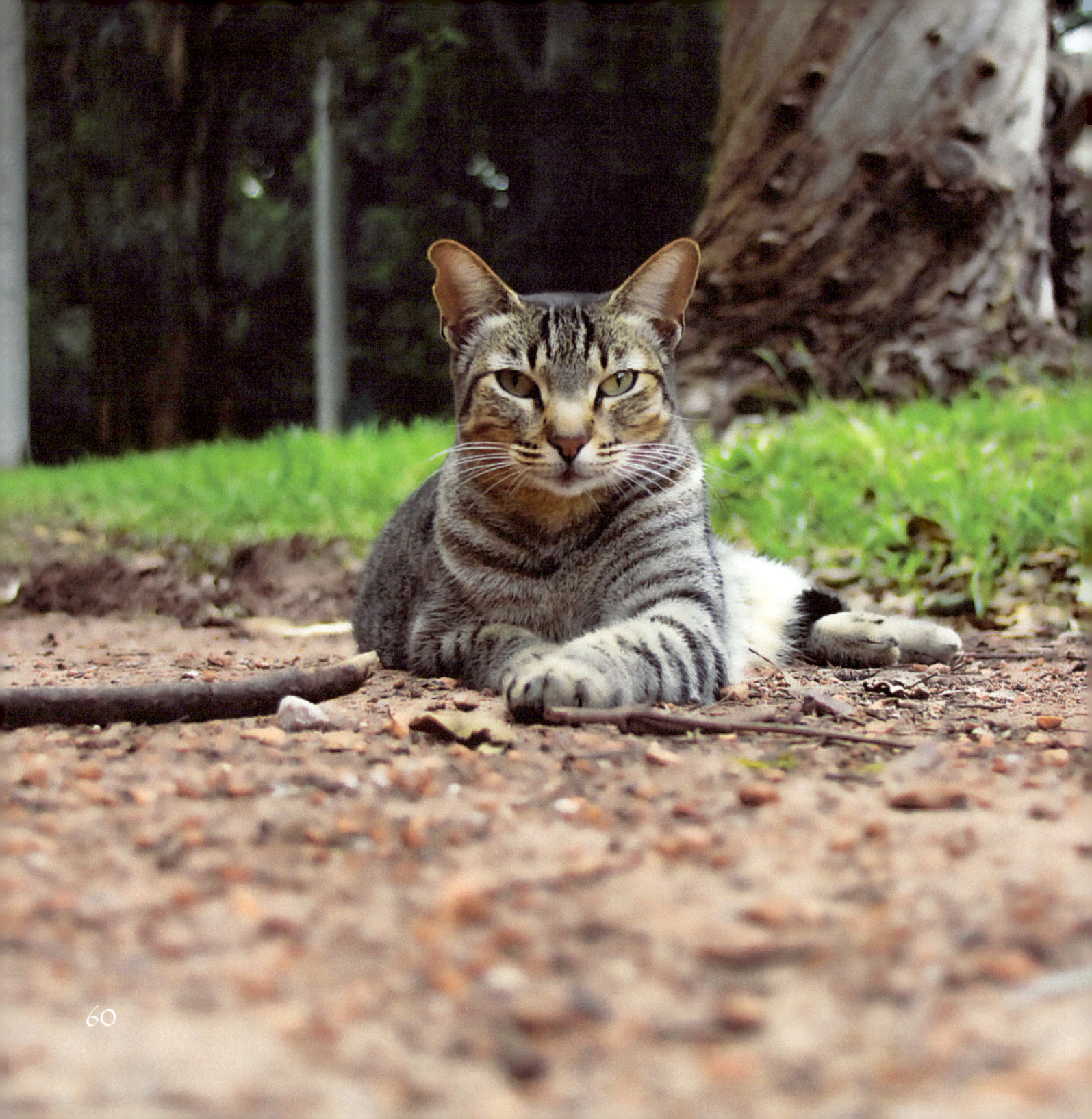

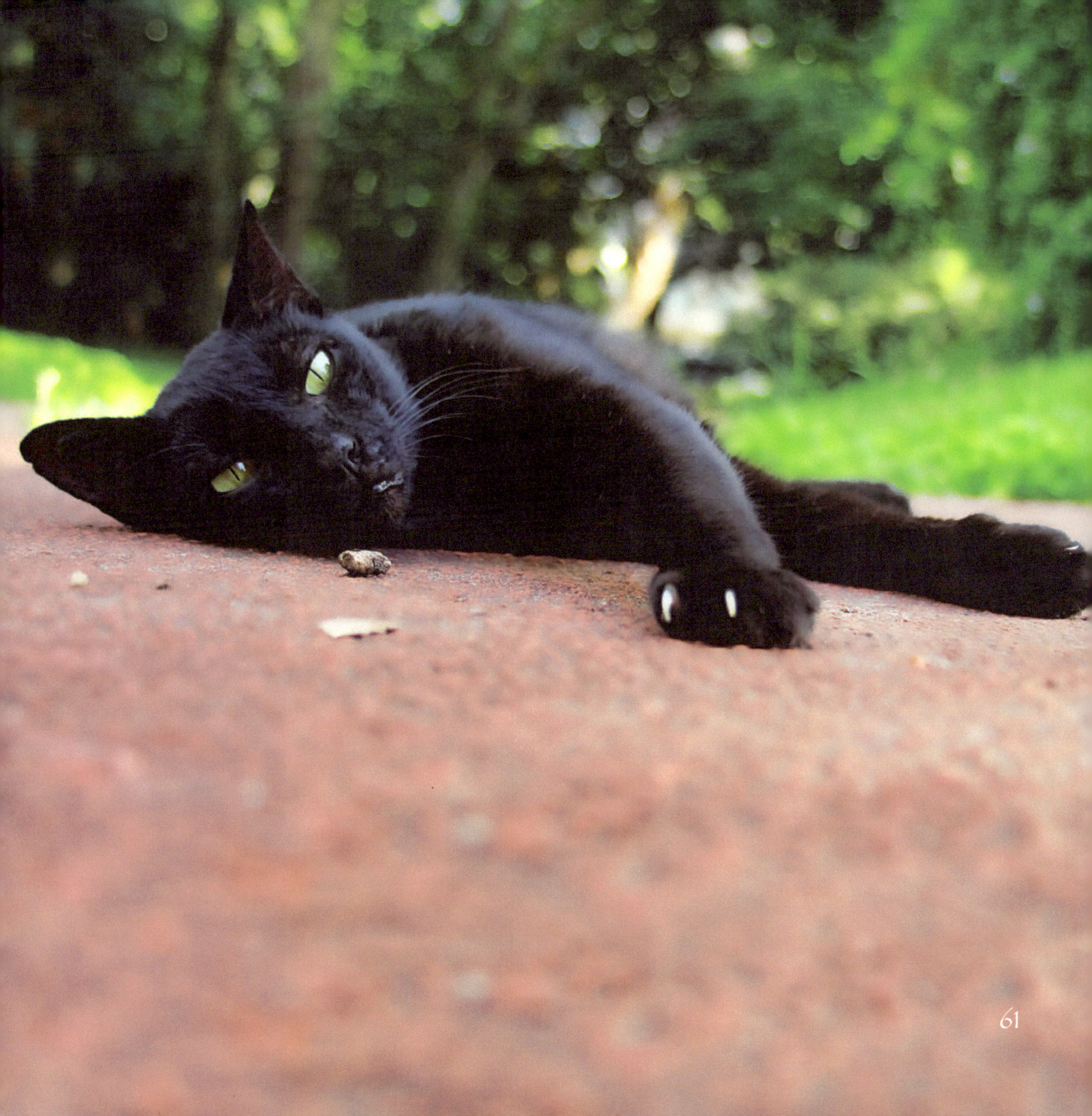

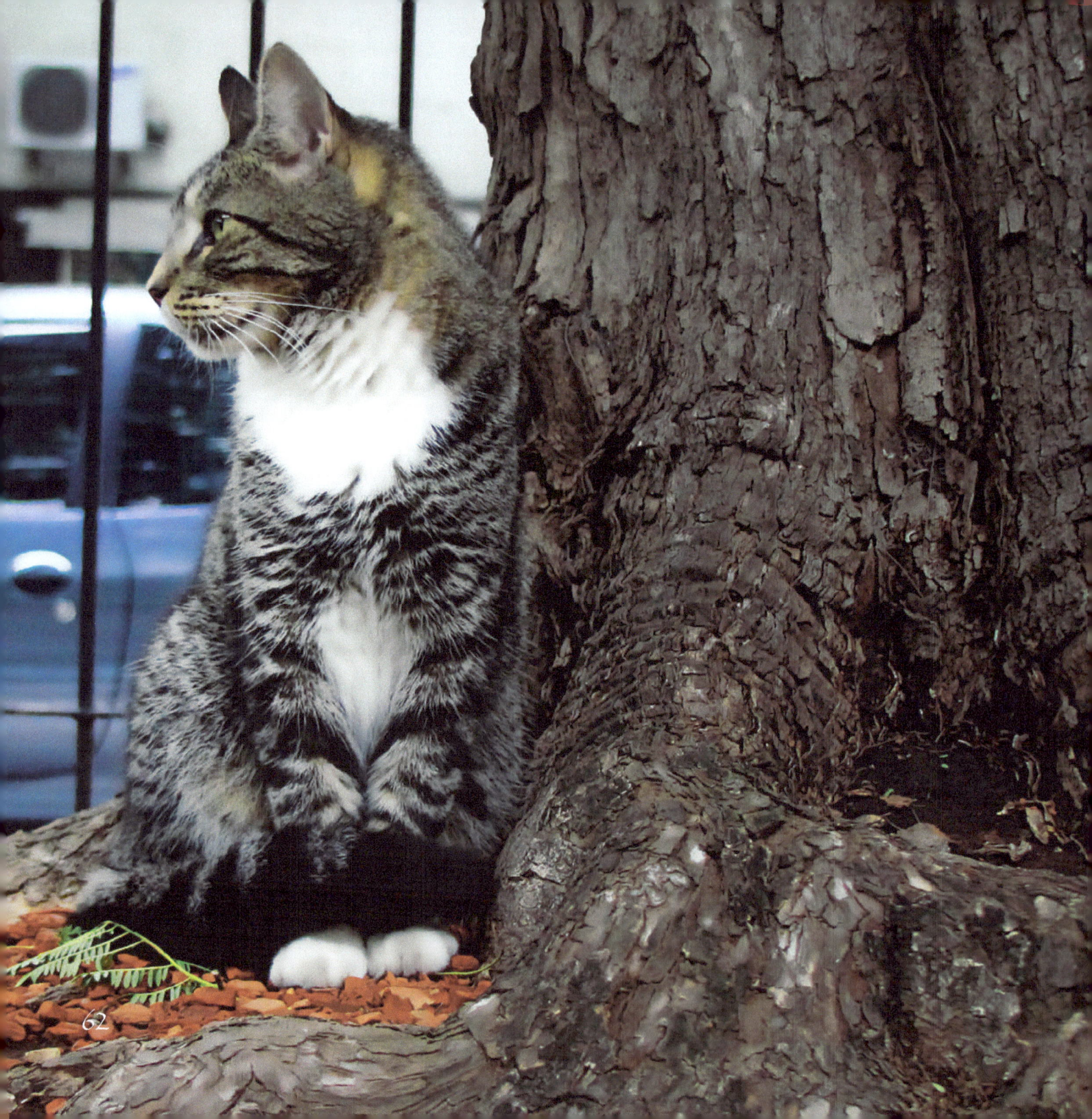

The Tango, the most elegant of dances, originated
in the brothels surrounding Buenos Aires

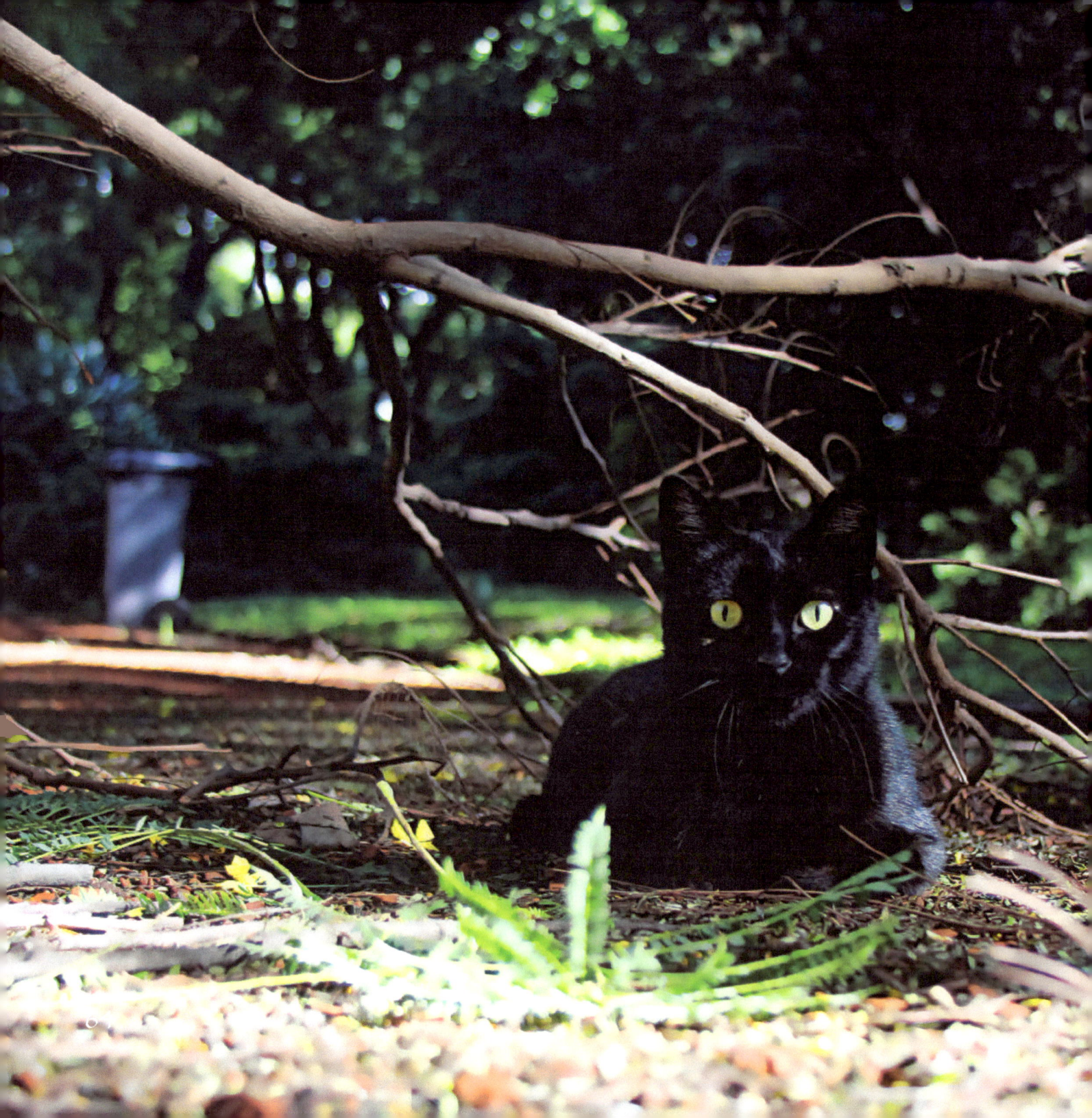

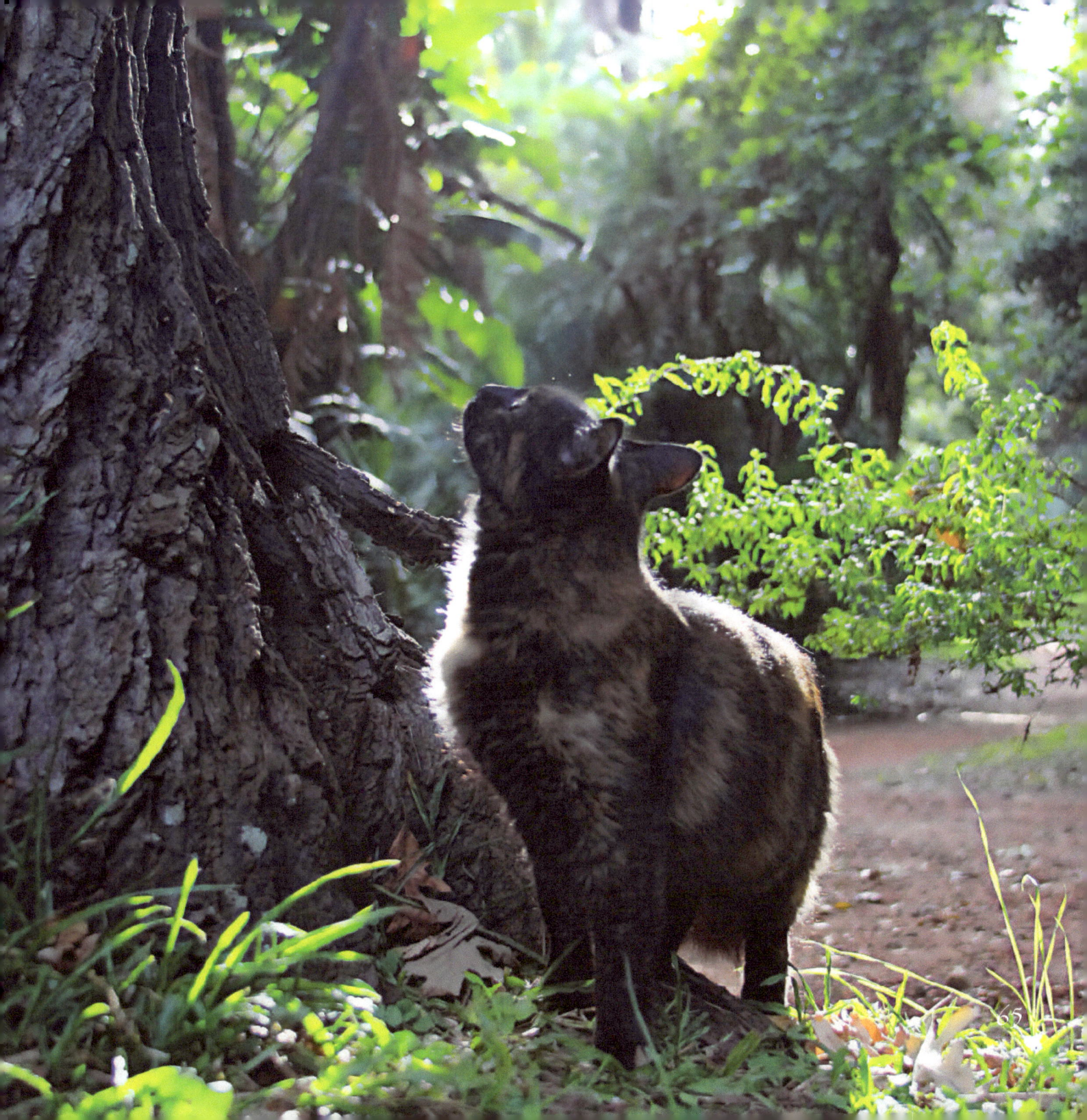

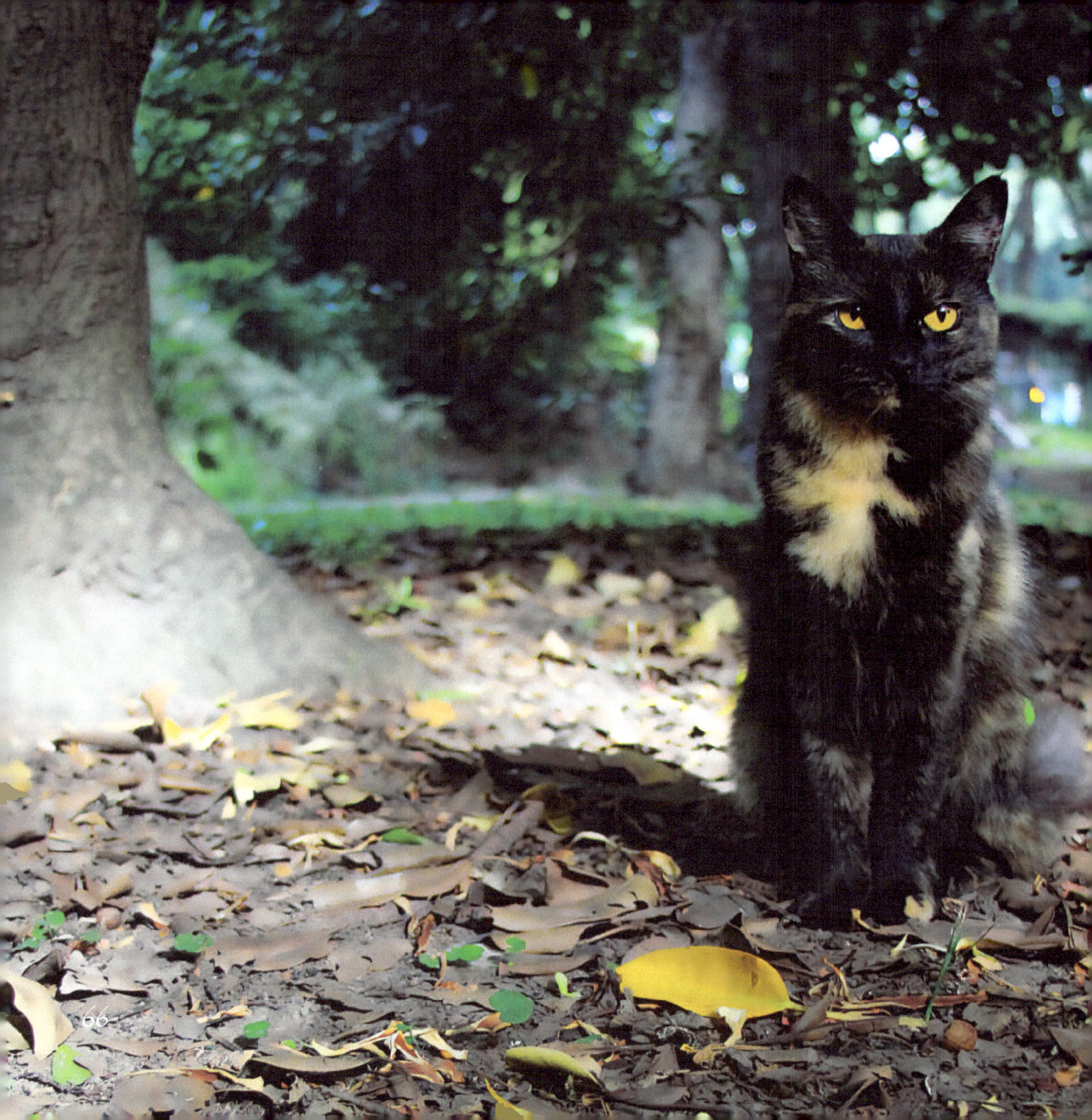

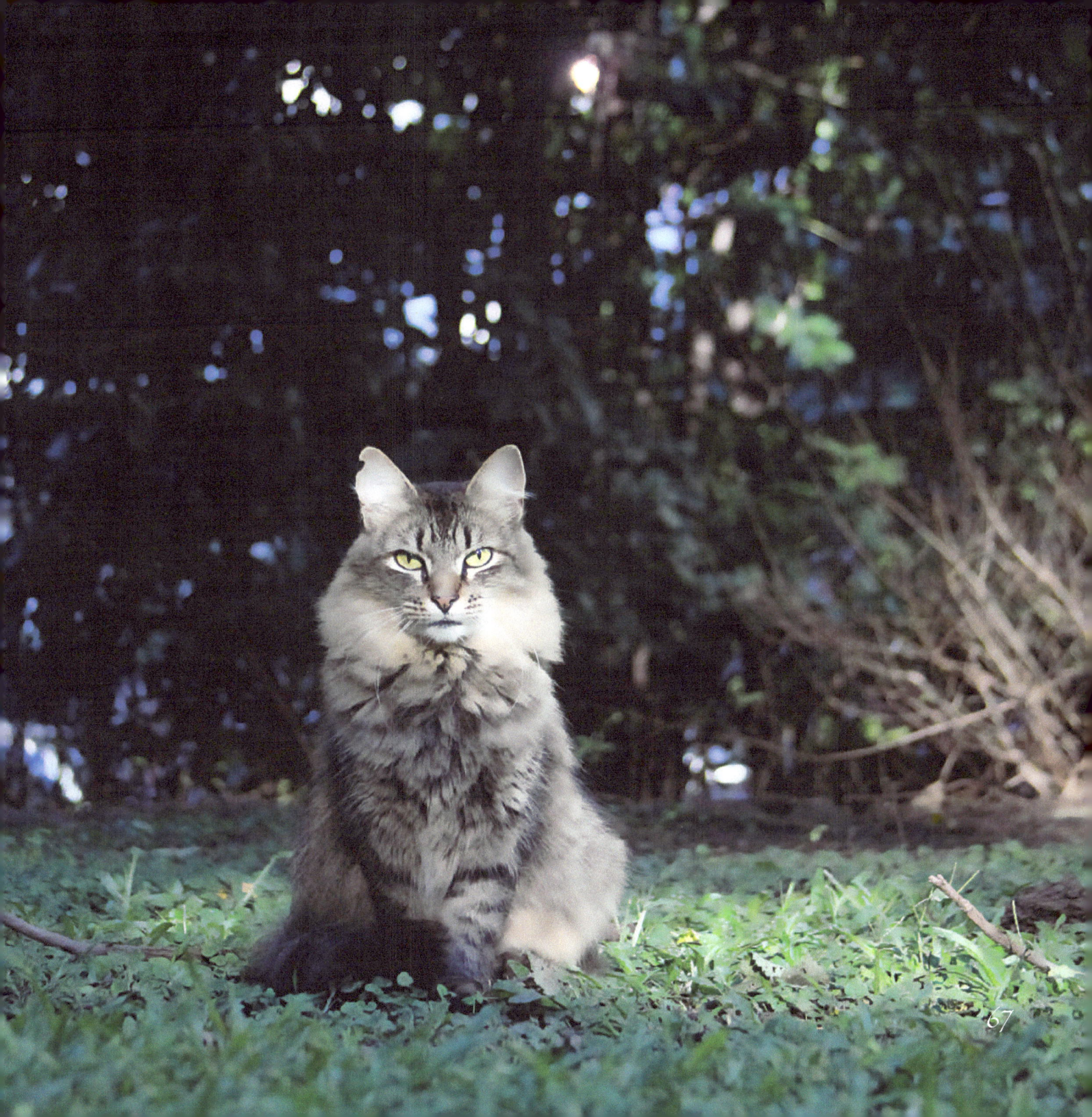

About 37% of American homes today have at least one cat

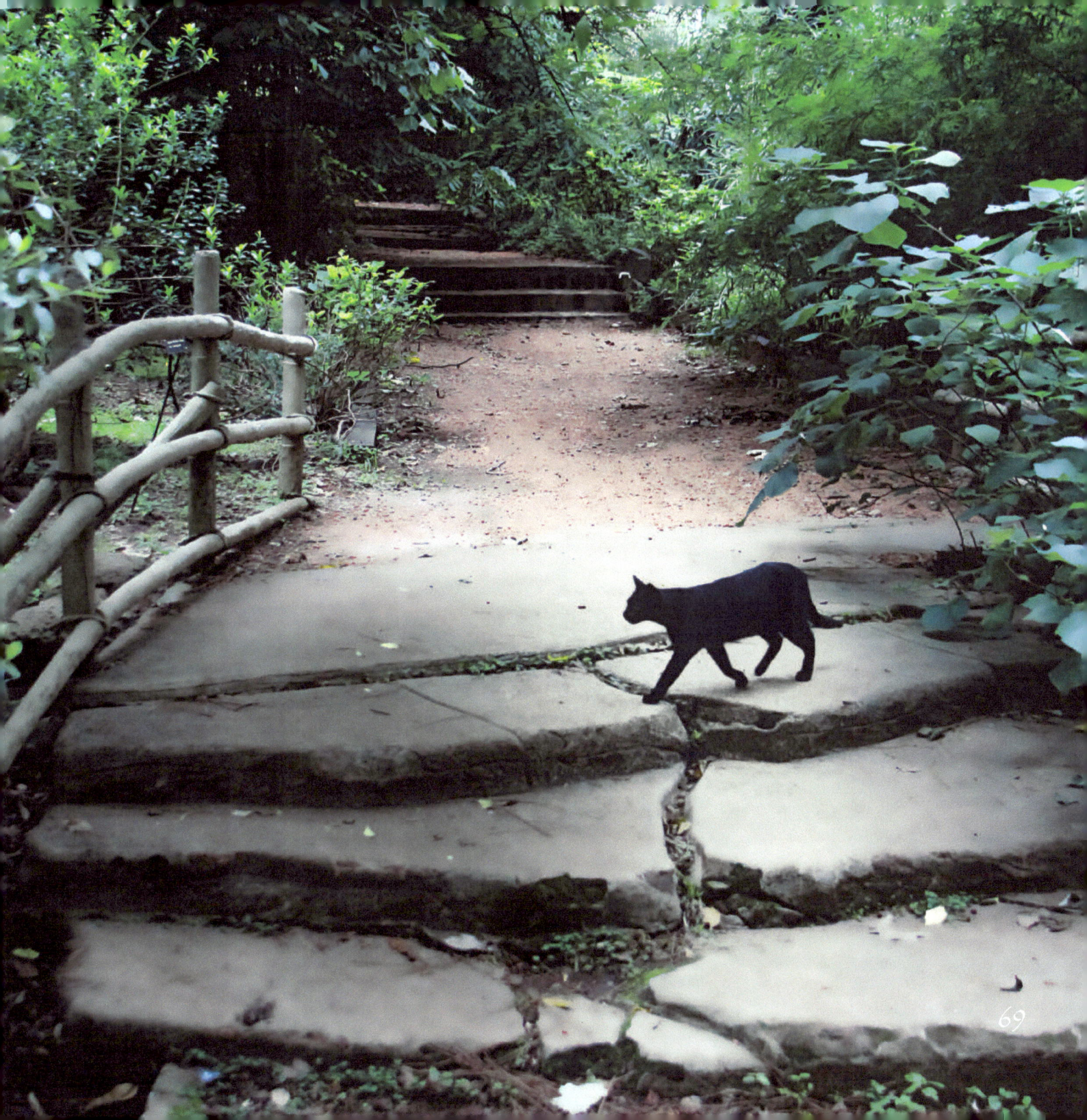

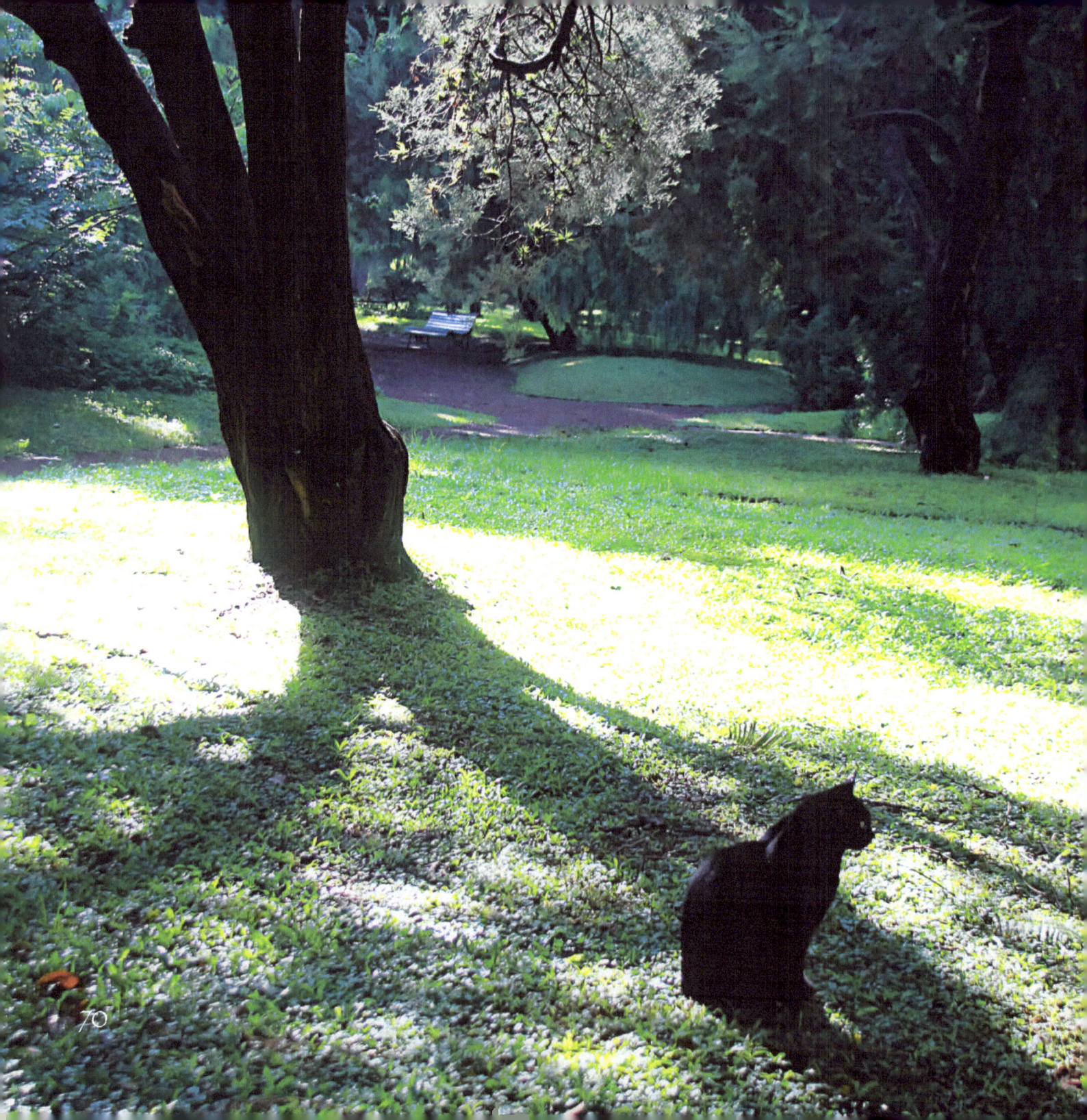

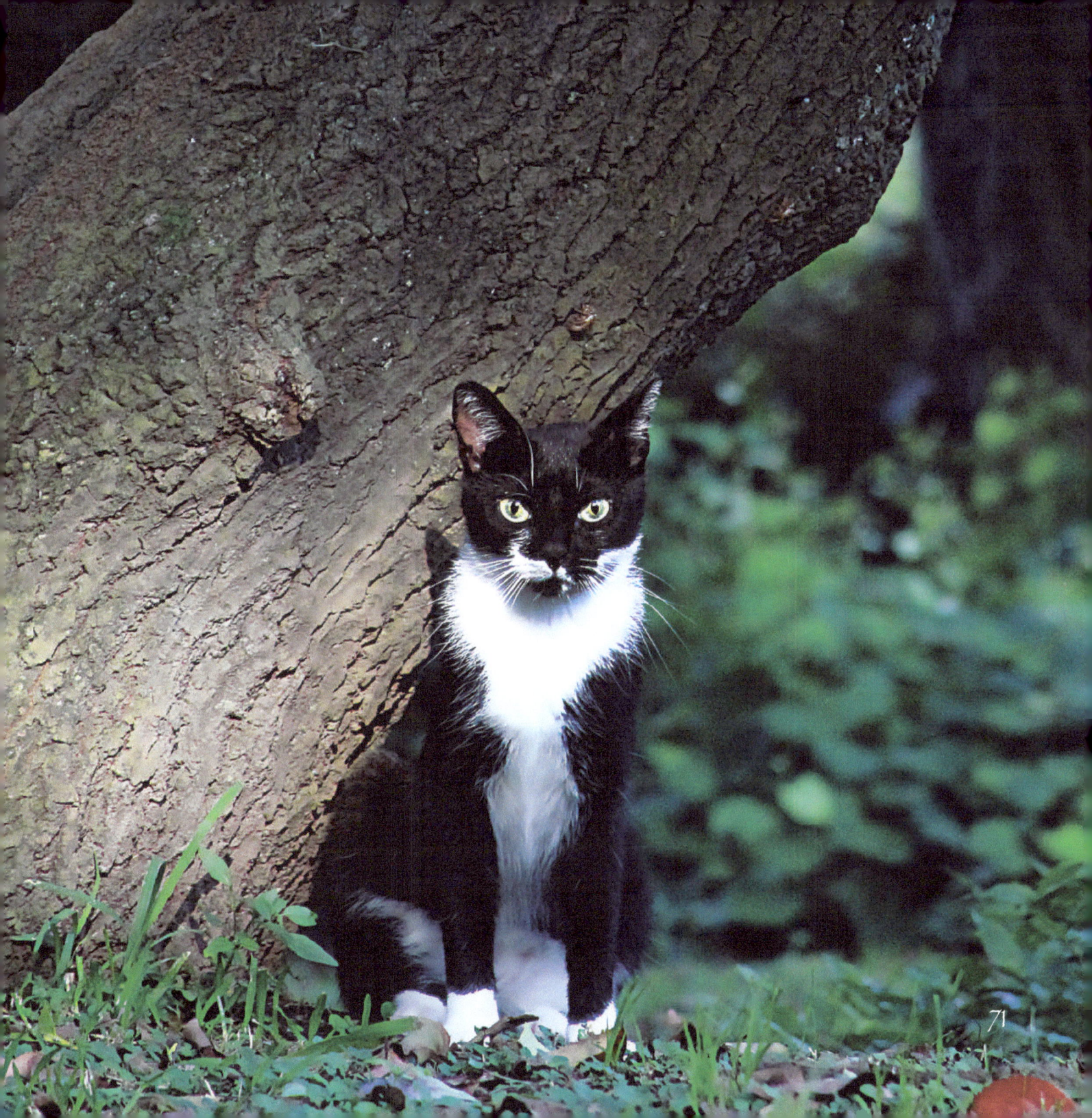

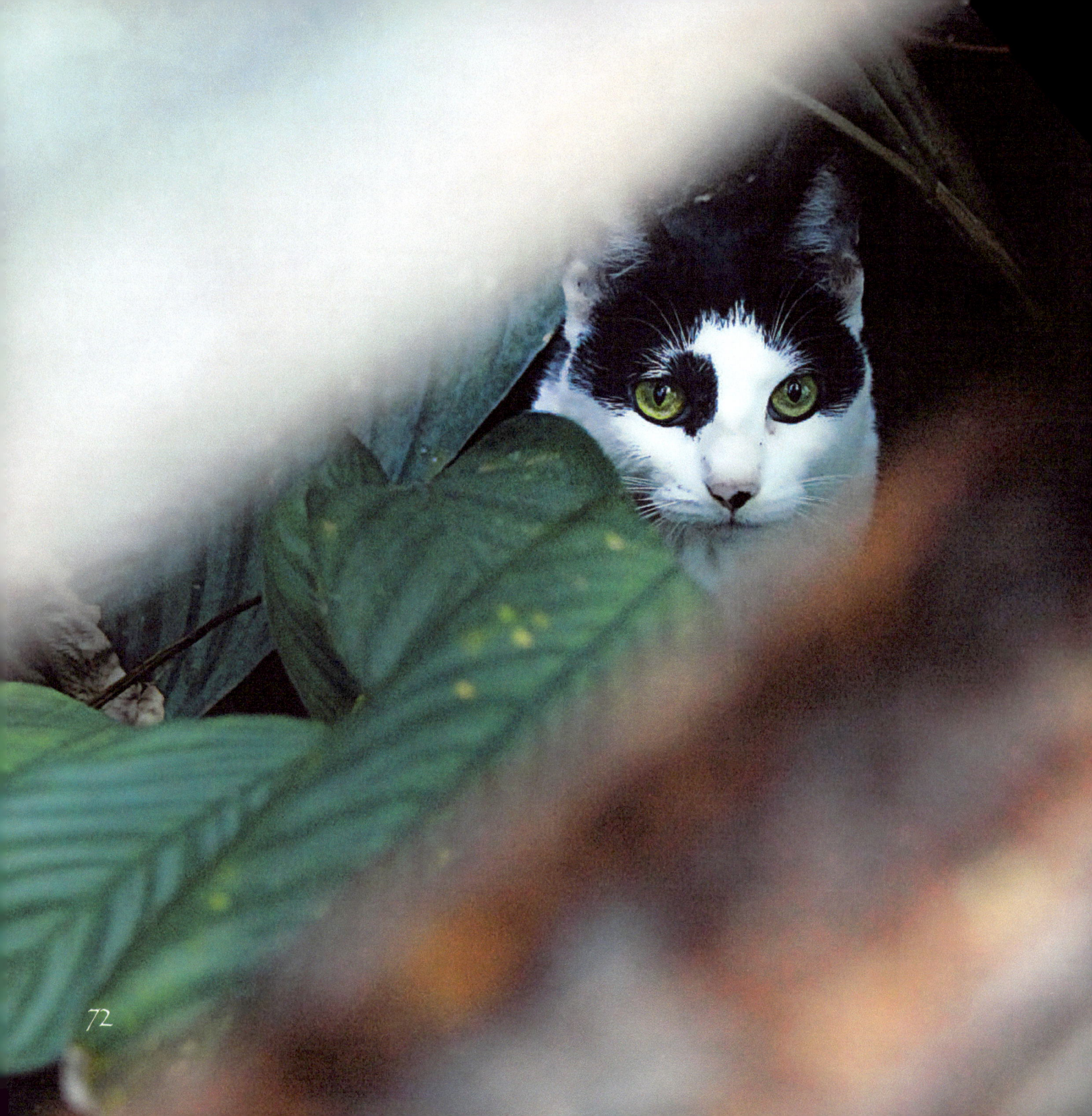

85 percent of Buenos Aires residents are of European descent consisting mostly of Italians, Germans, and Spaniards

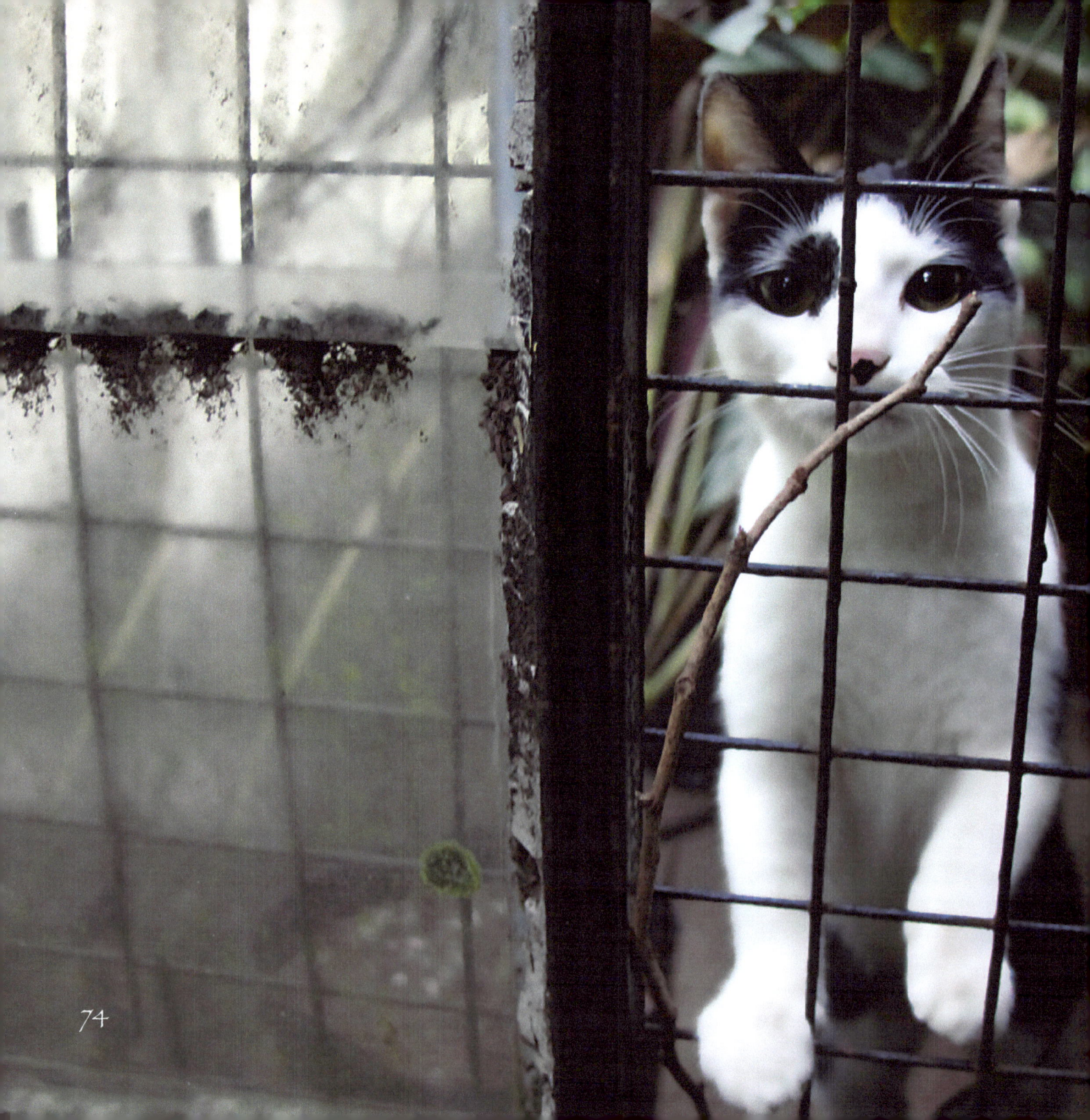

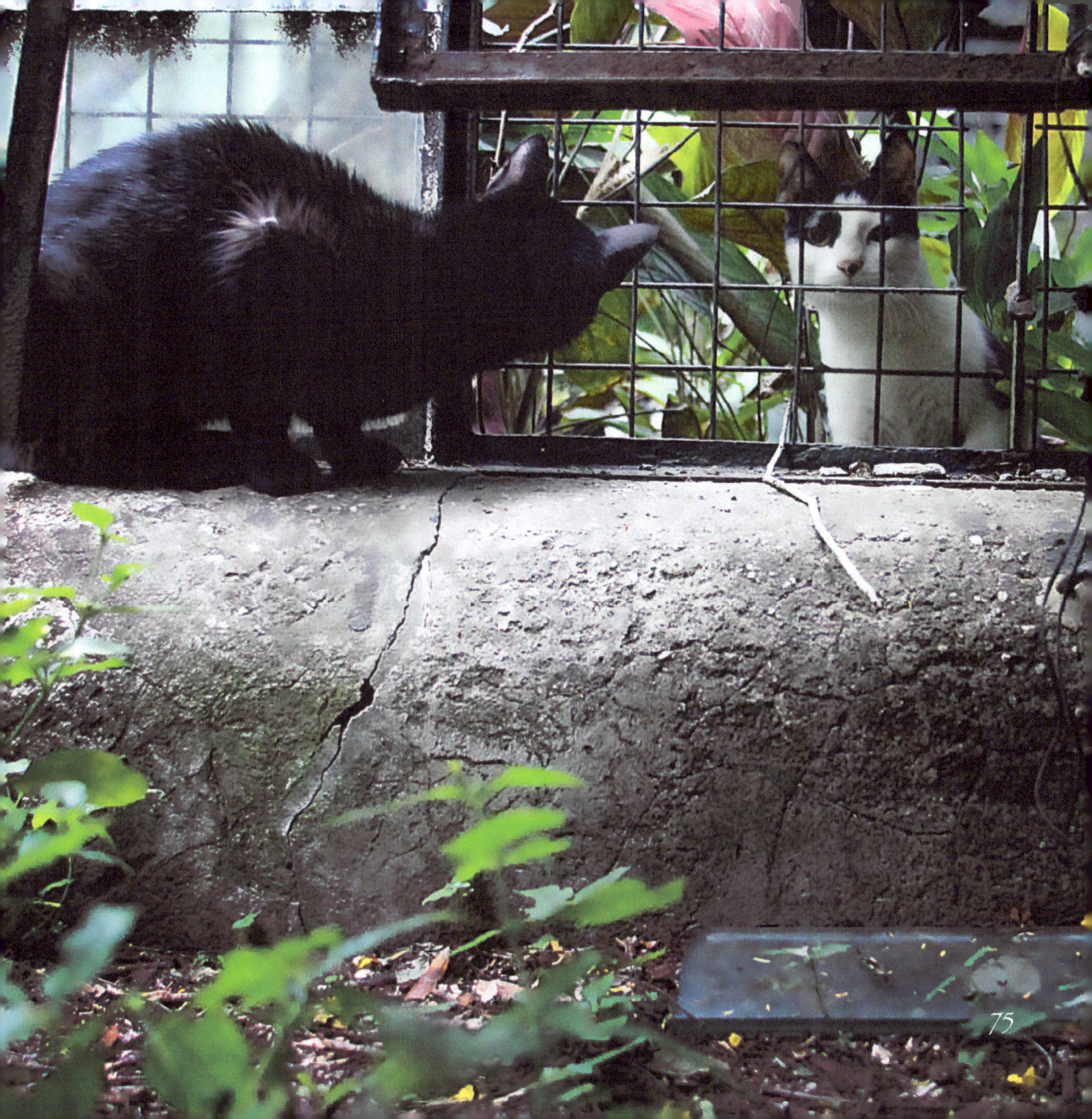

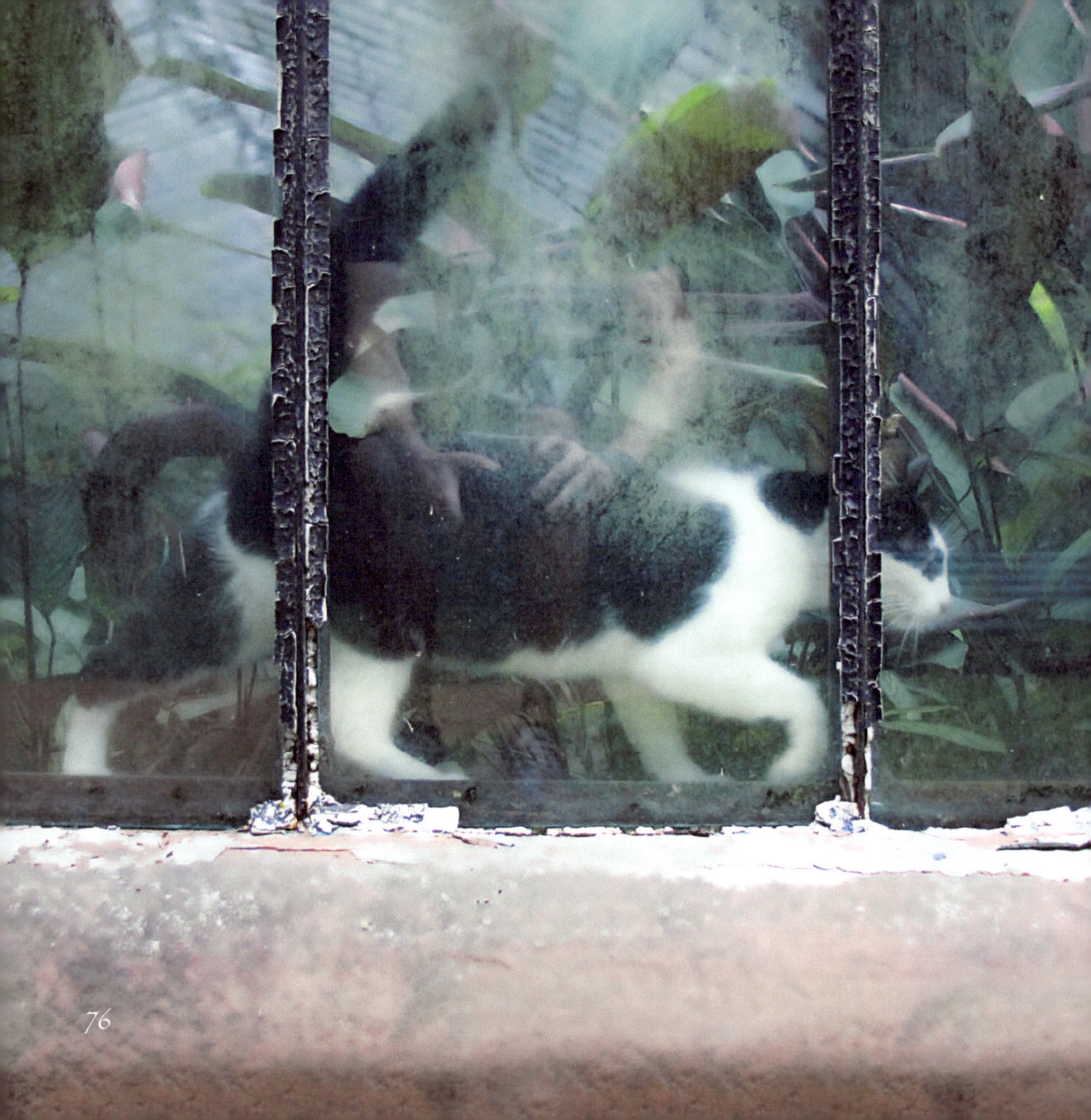

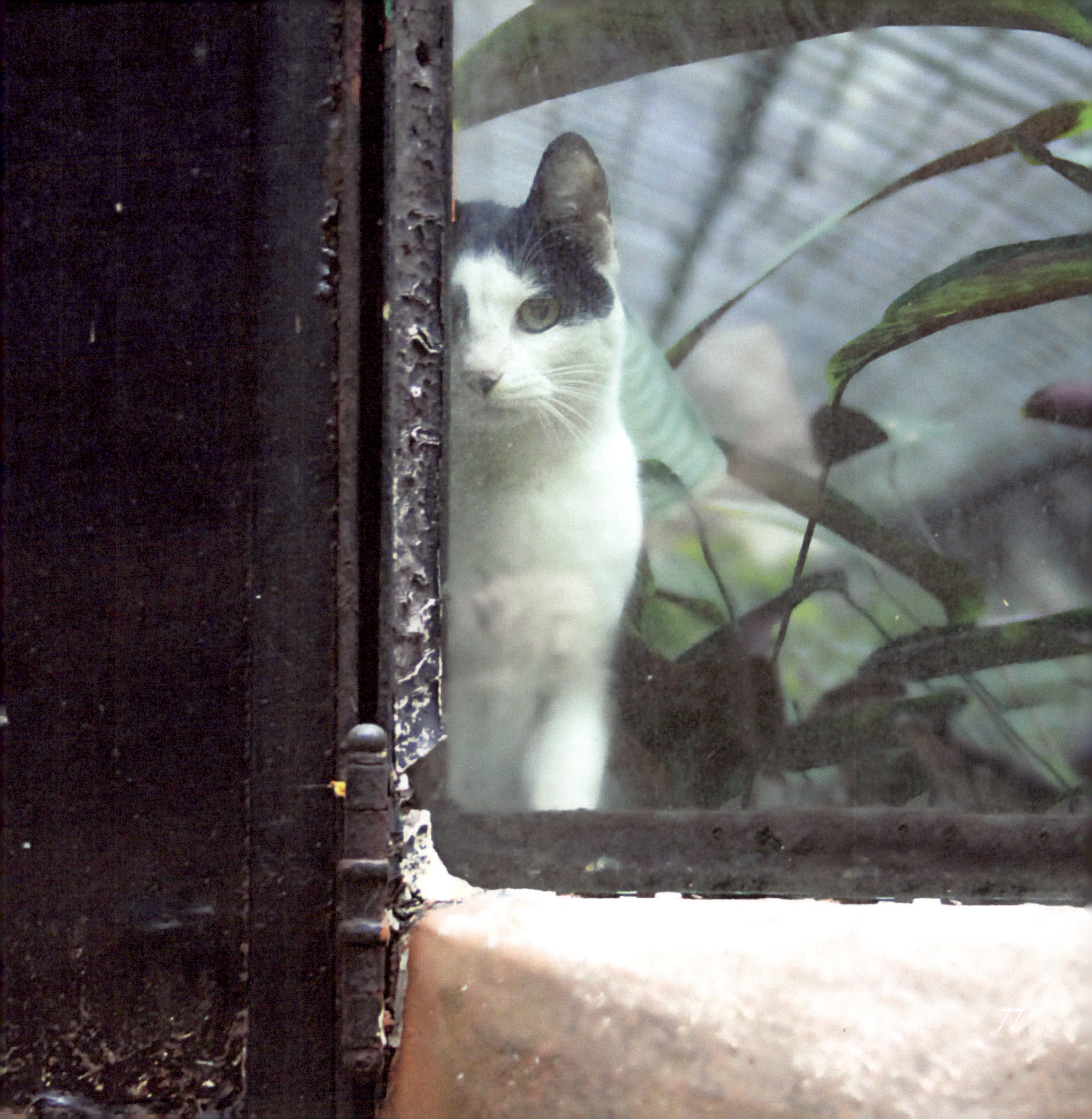

The biggest wildcat today is the Siberian Tiger it can be more than 12 feet long and weigh up to 700 pound

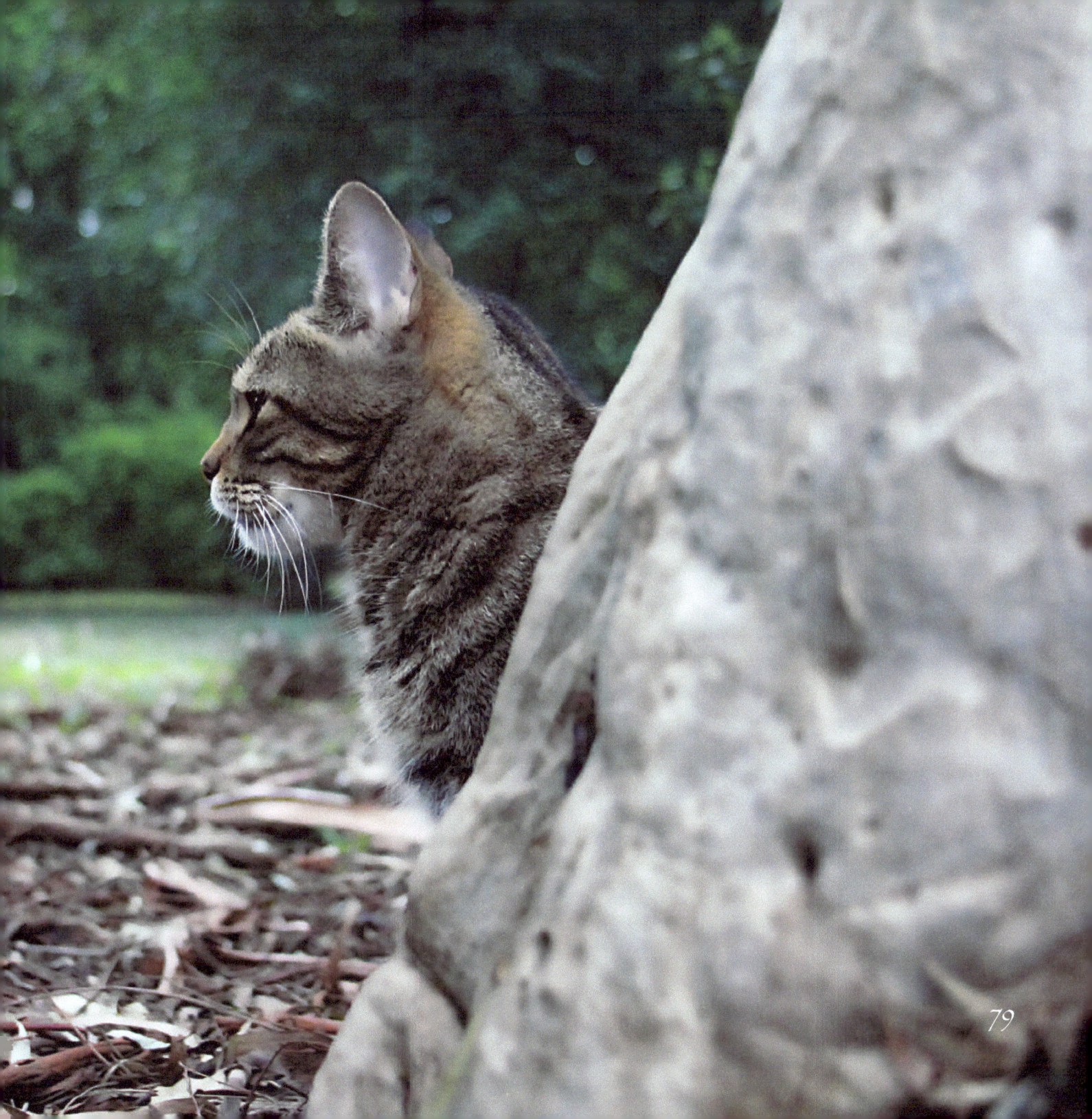

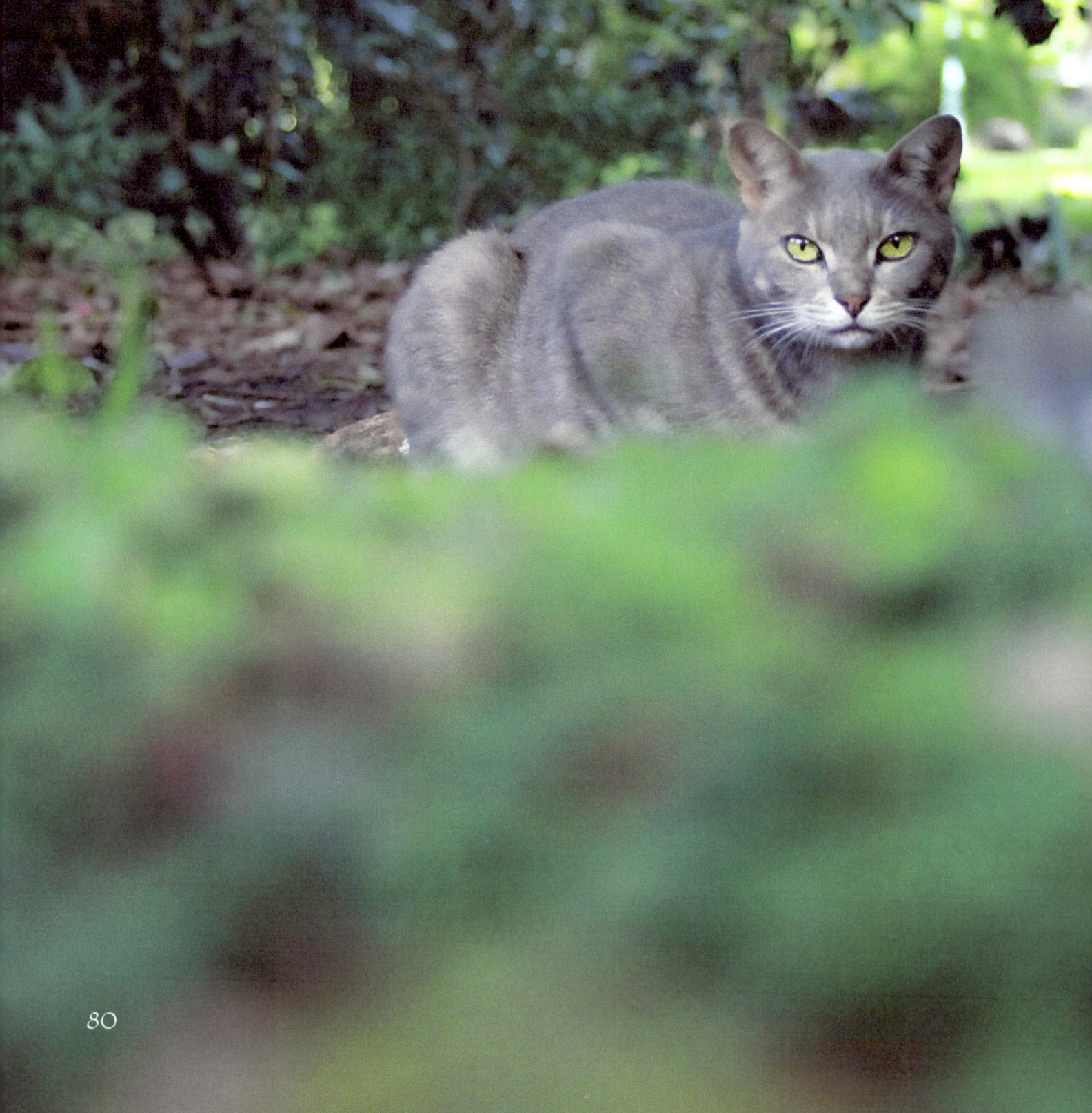

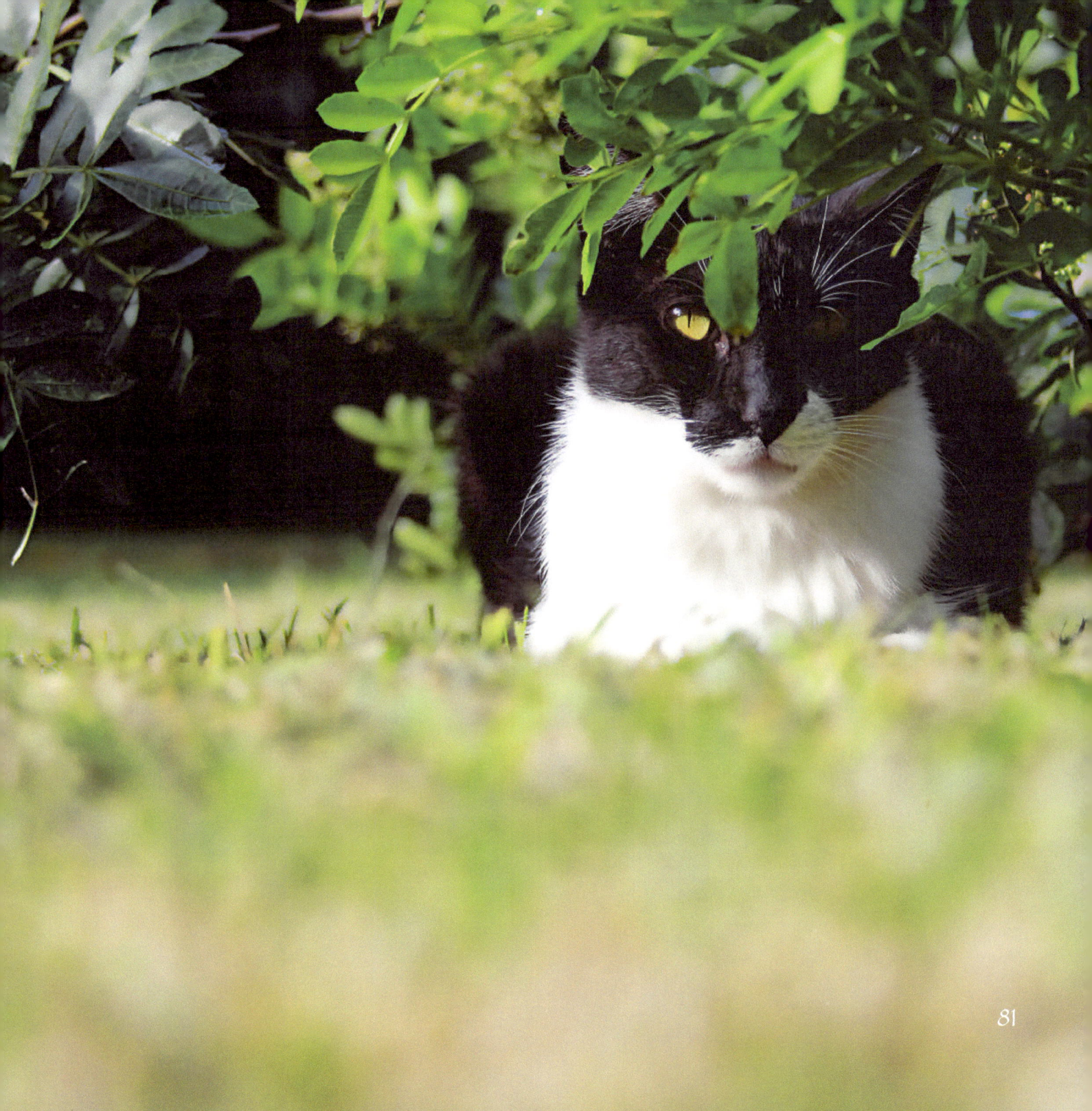

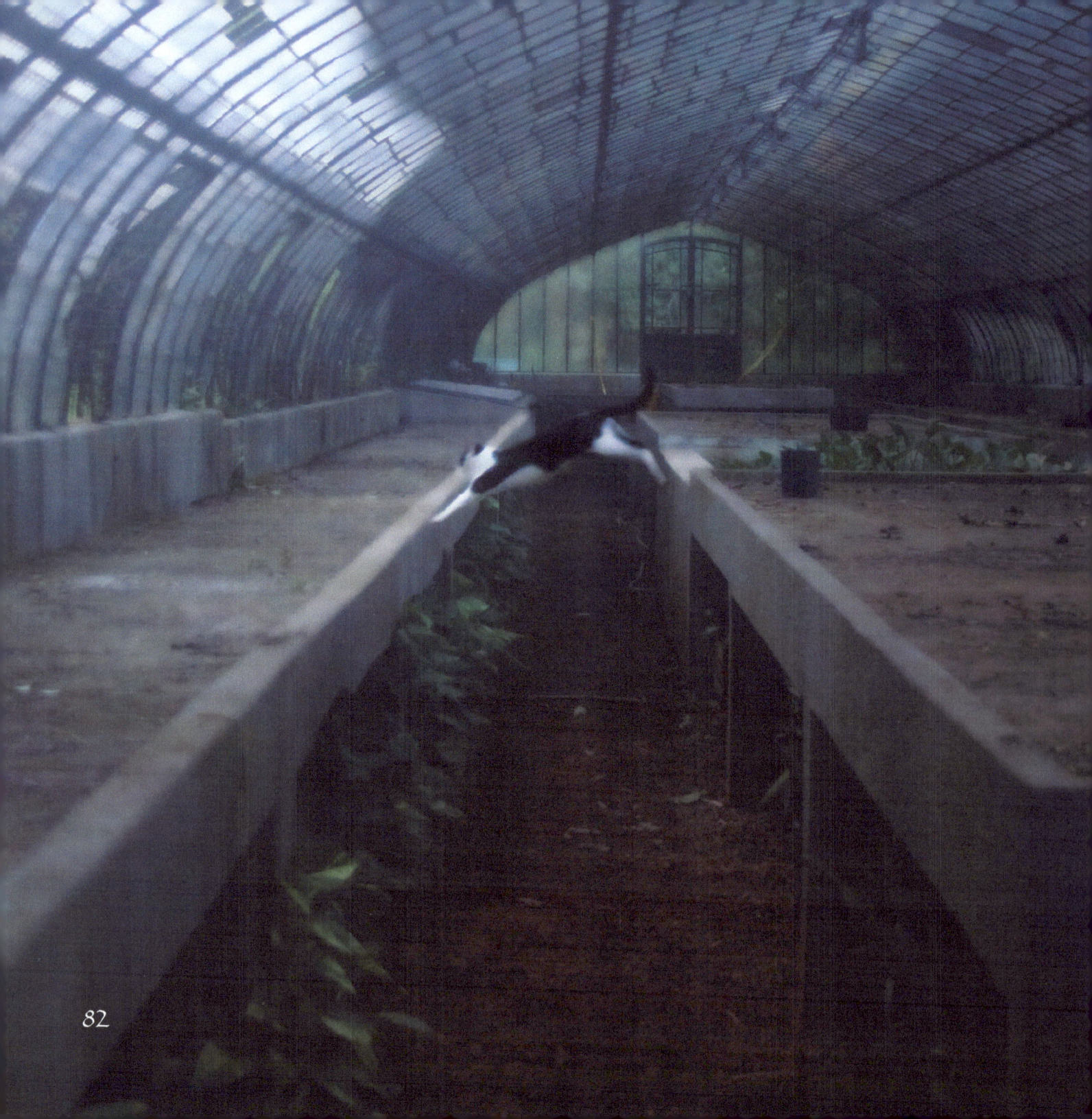

Residents of Buenos Aires speak a Spanish dialect infused with an Italian slang, which sounds more like Neapolitan Italian than Spanish

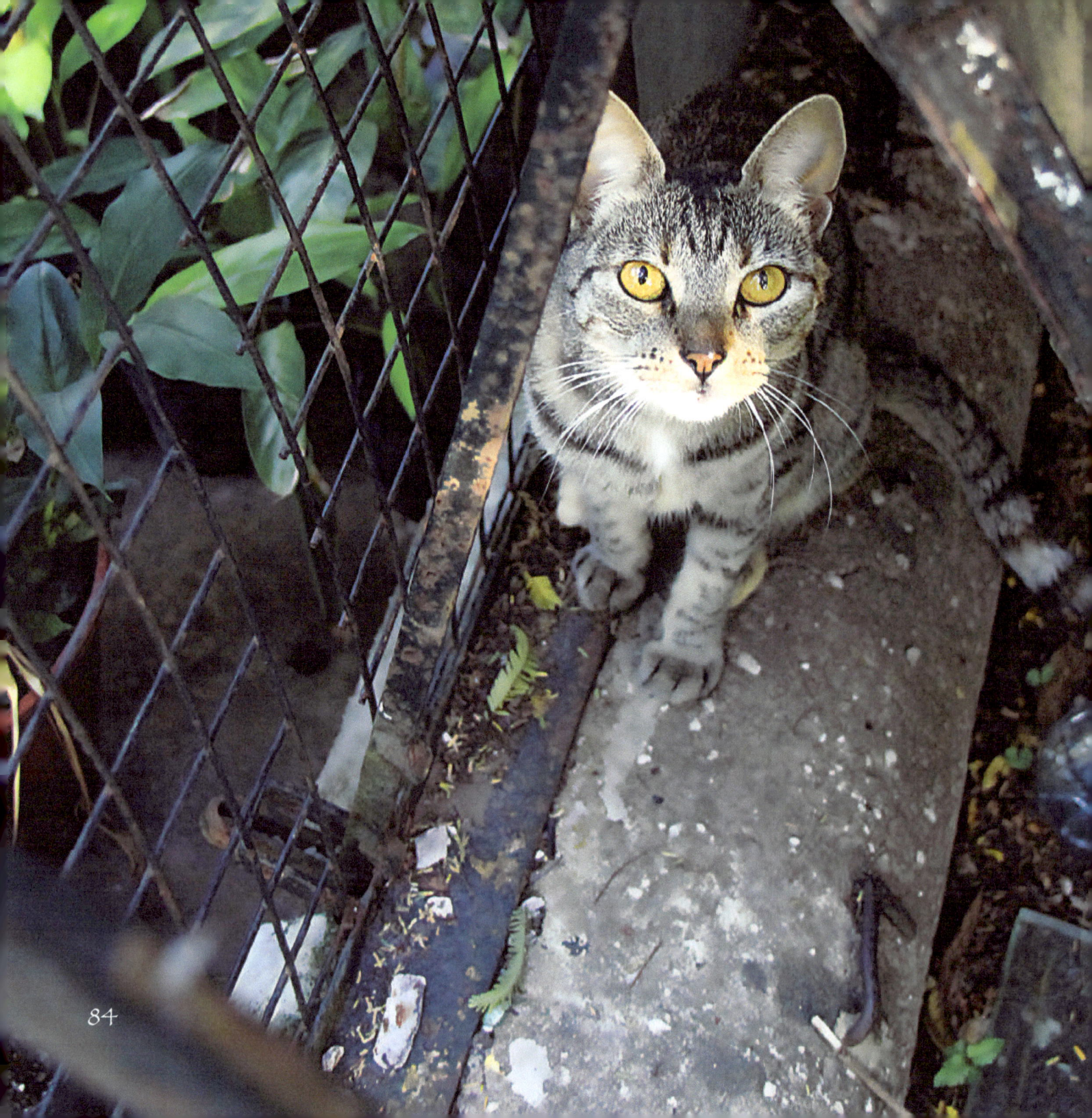

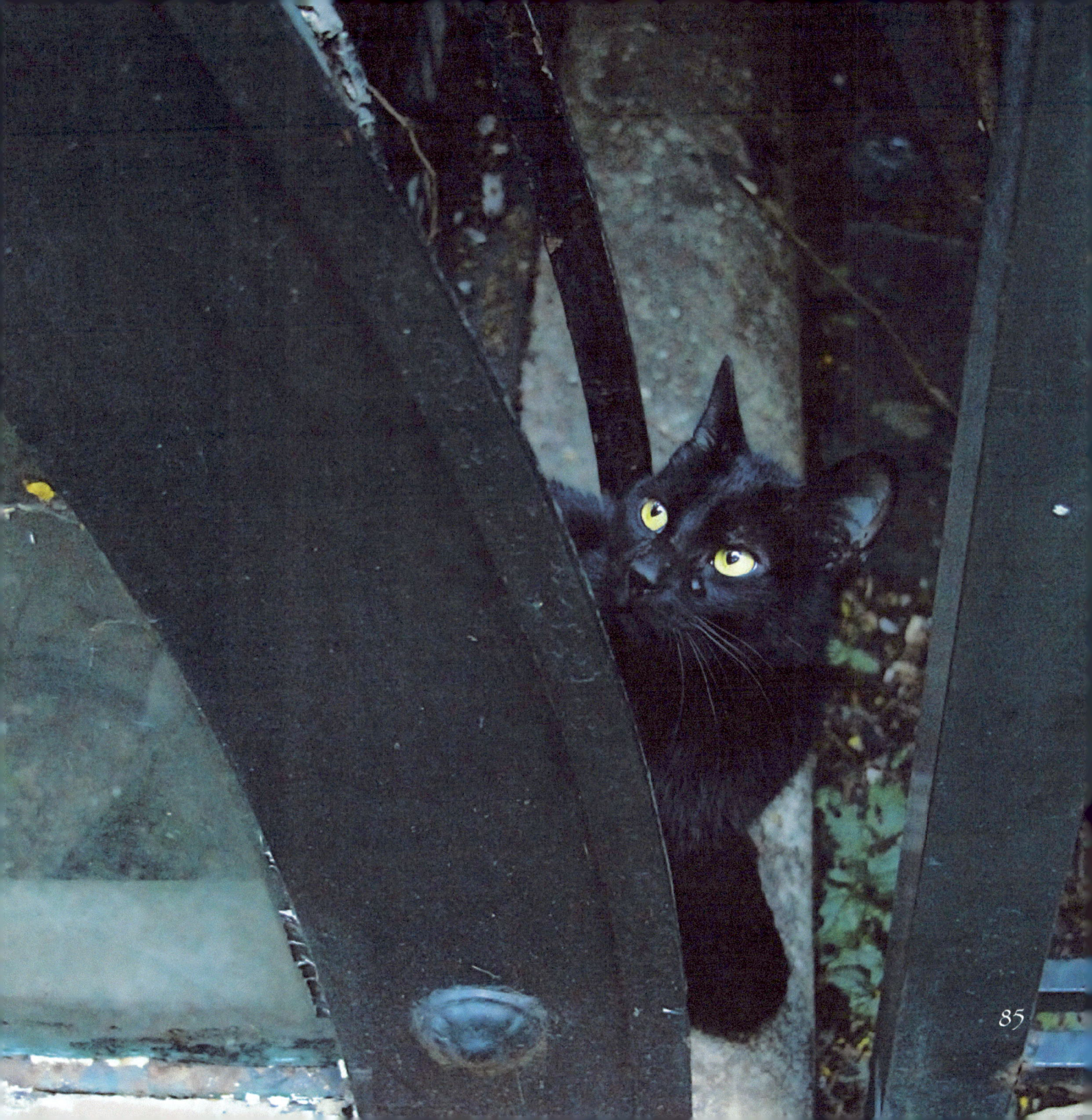

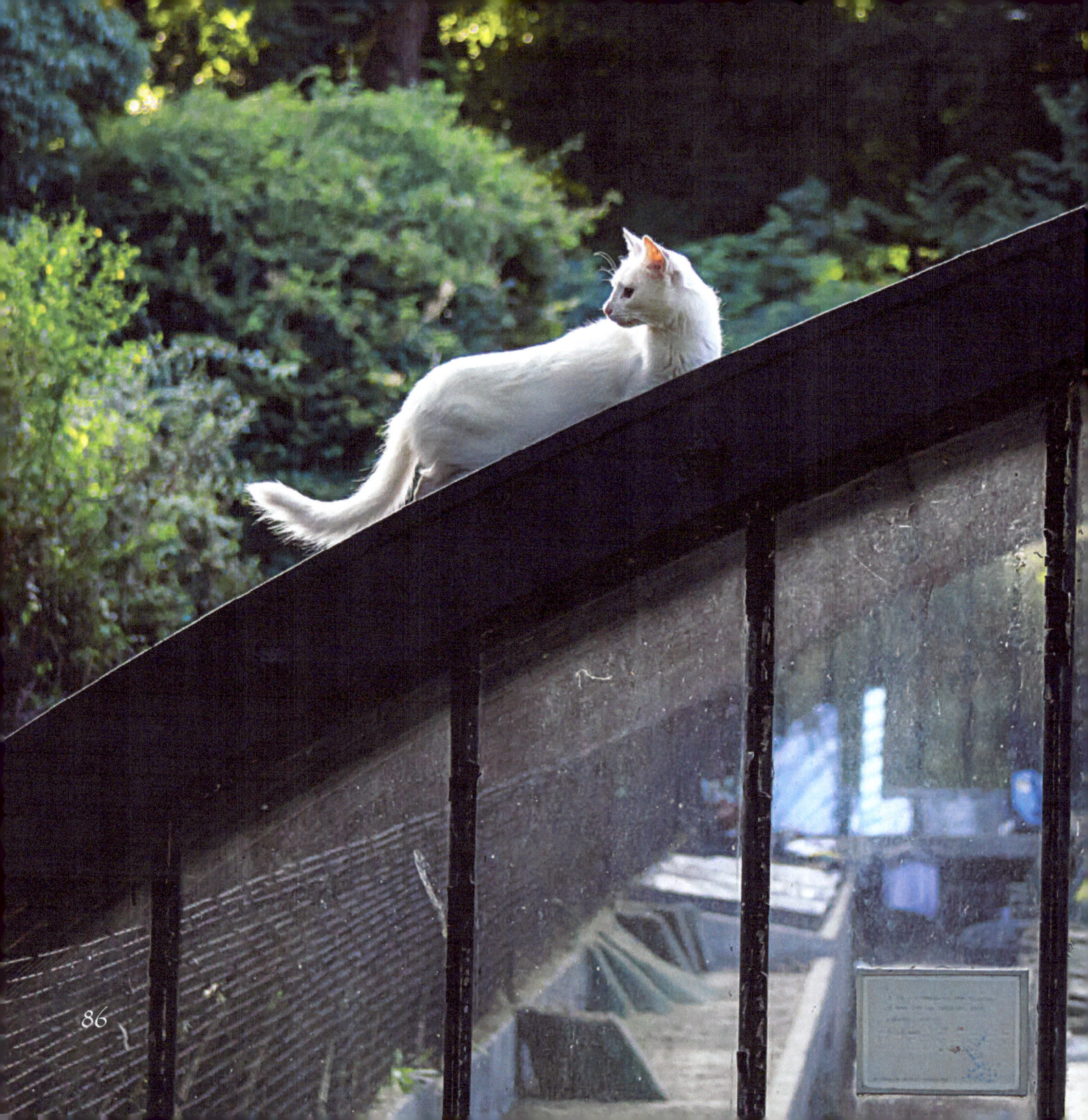

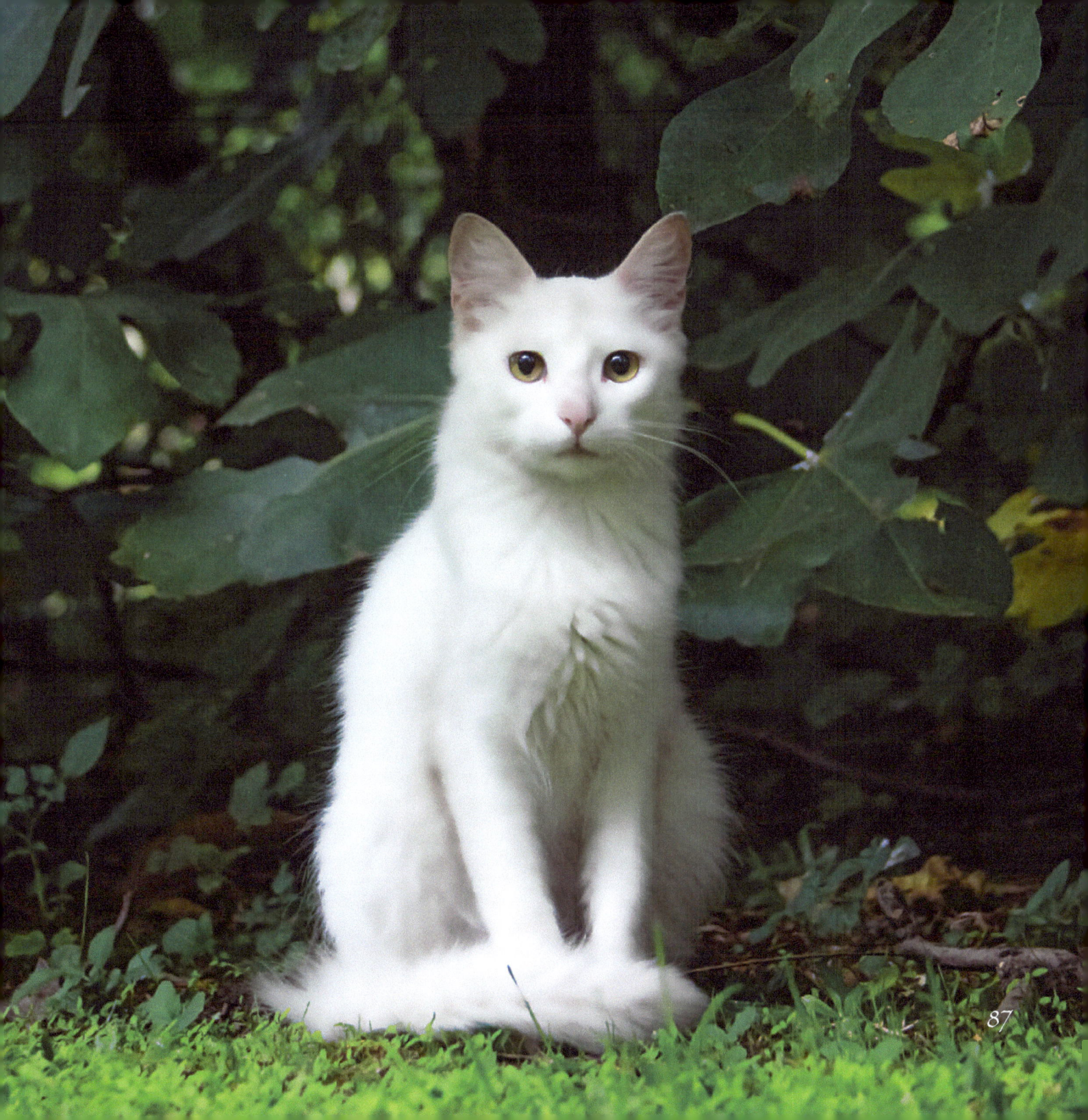

A cat has four rows of whiskers on each side

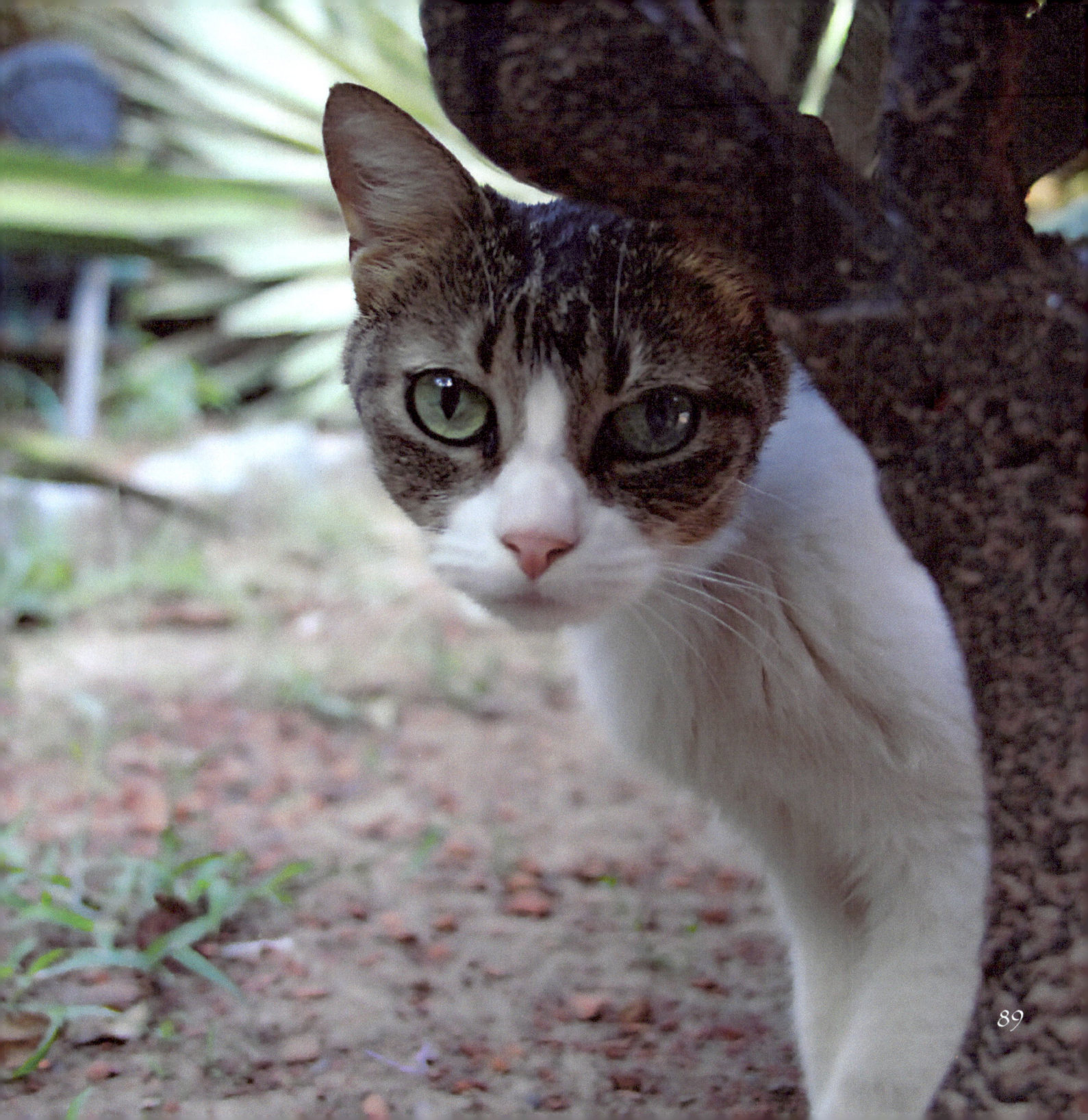

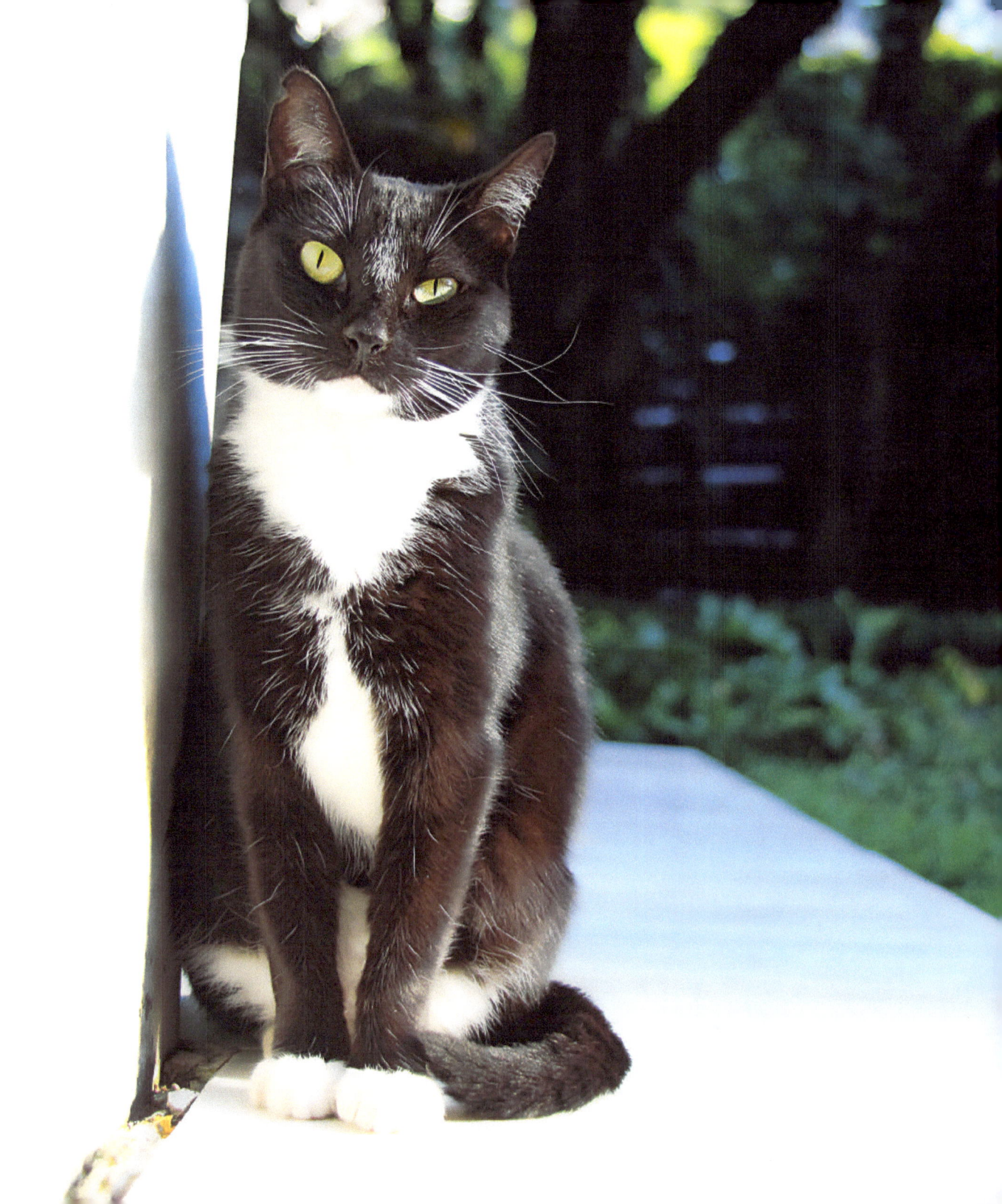

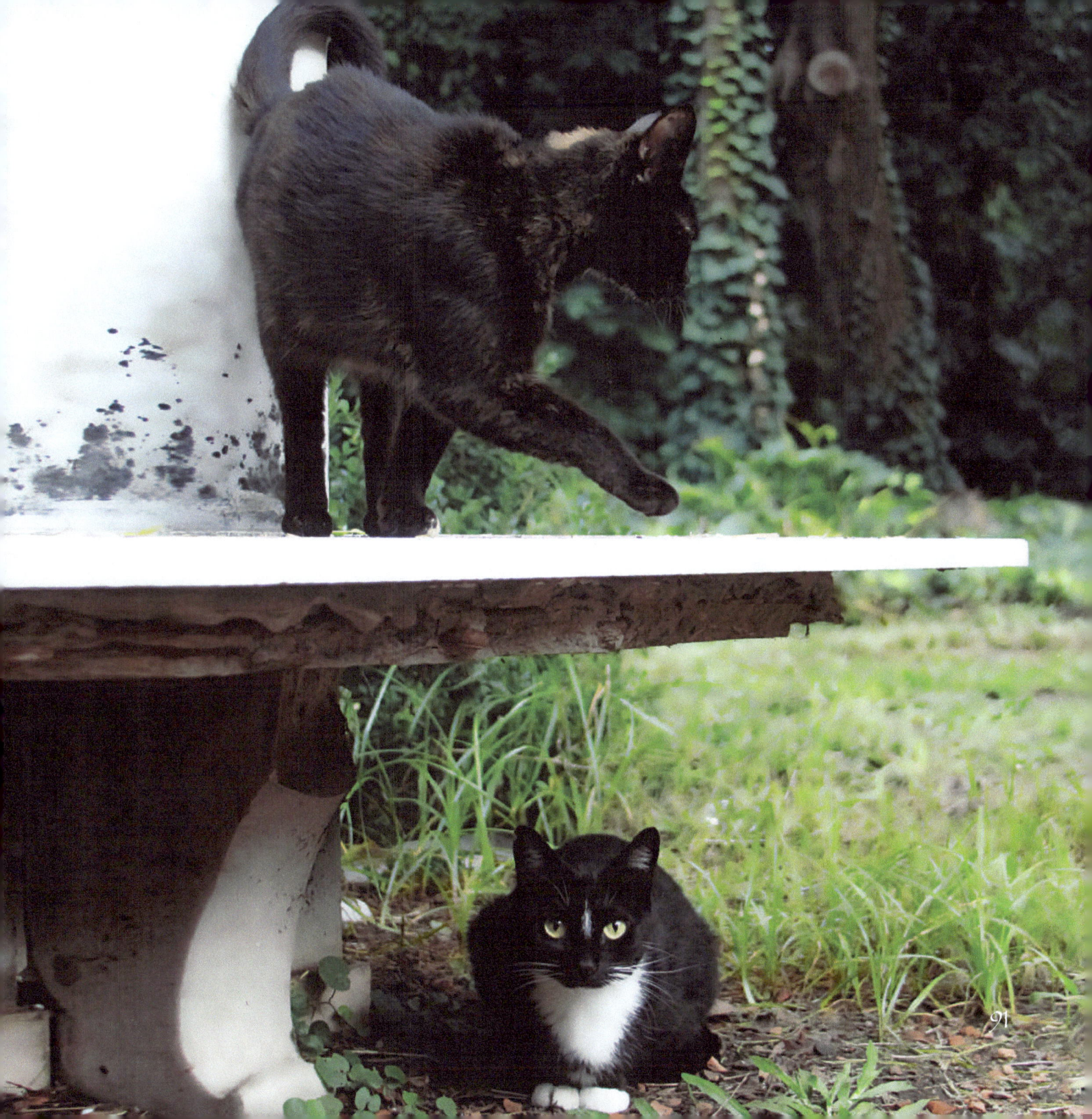

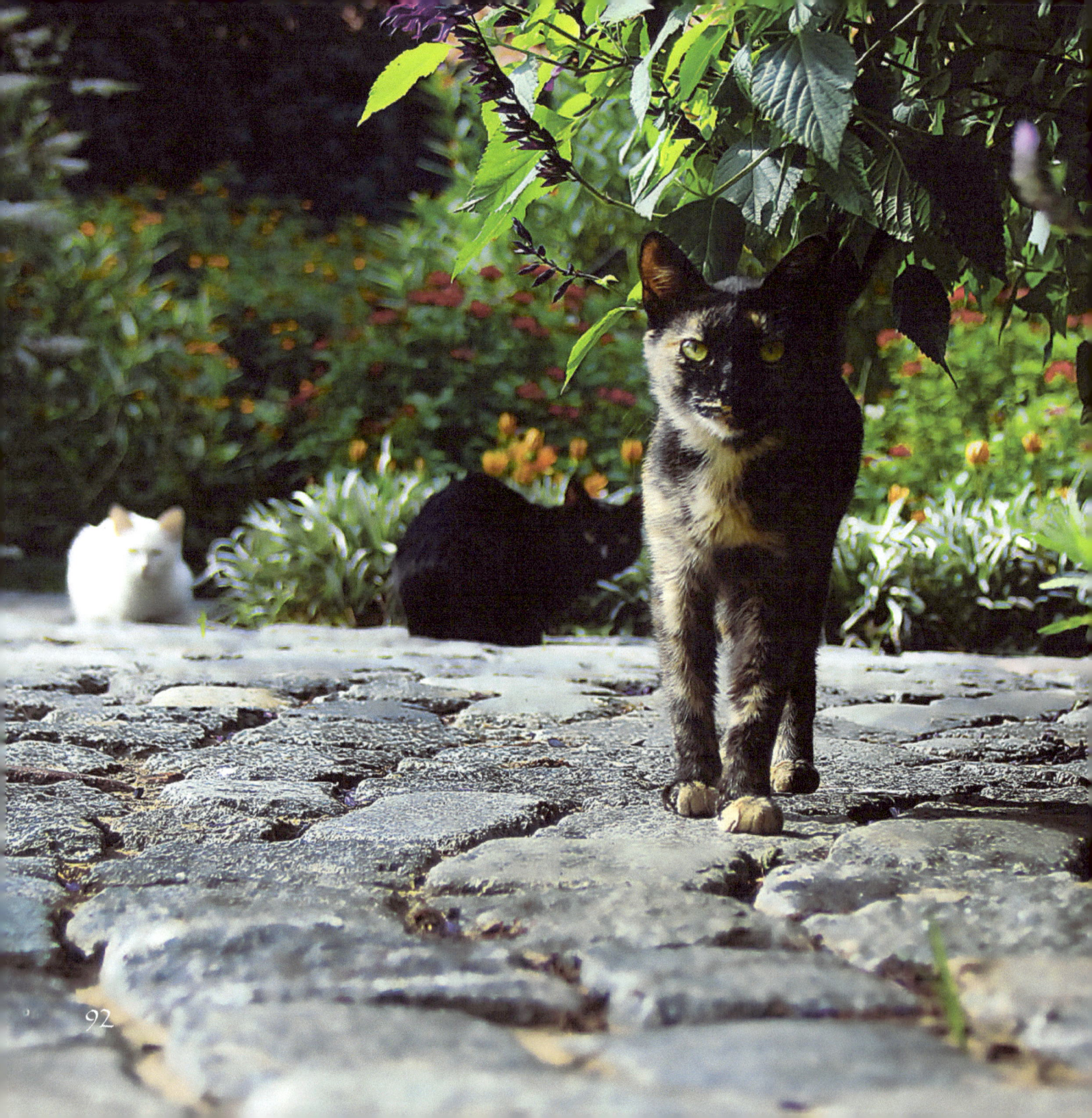

Buenos Aires is a soccer-obsessed town and is home to one of the highest concentrations of professional teams in the world

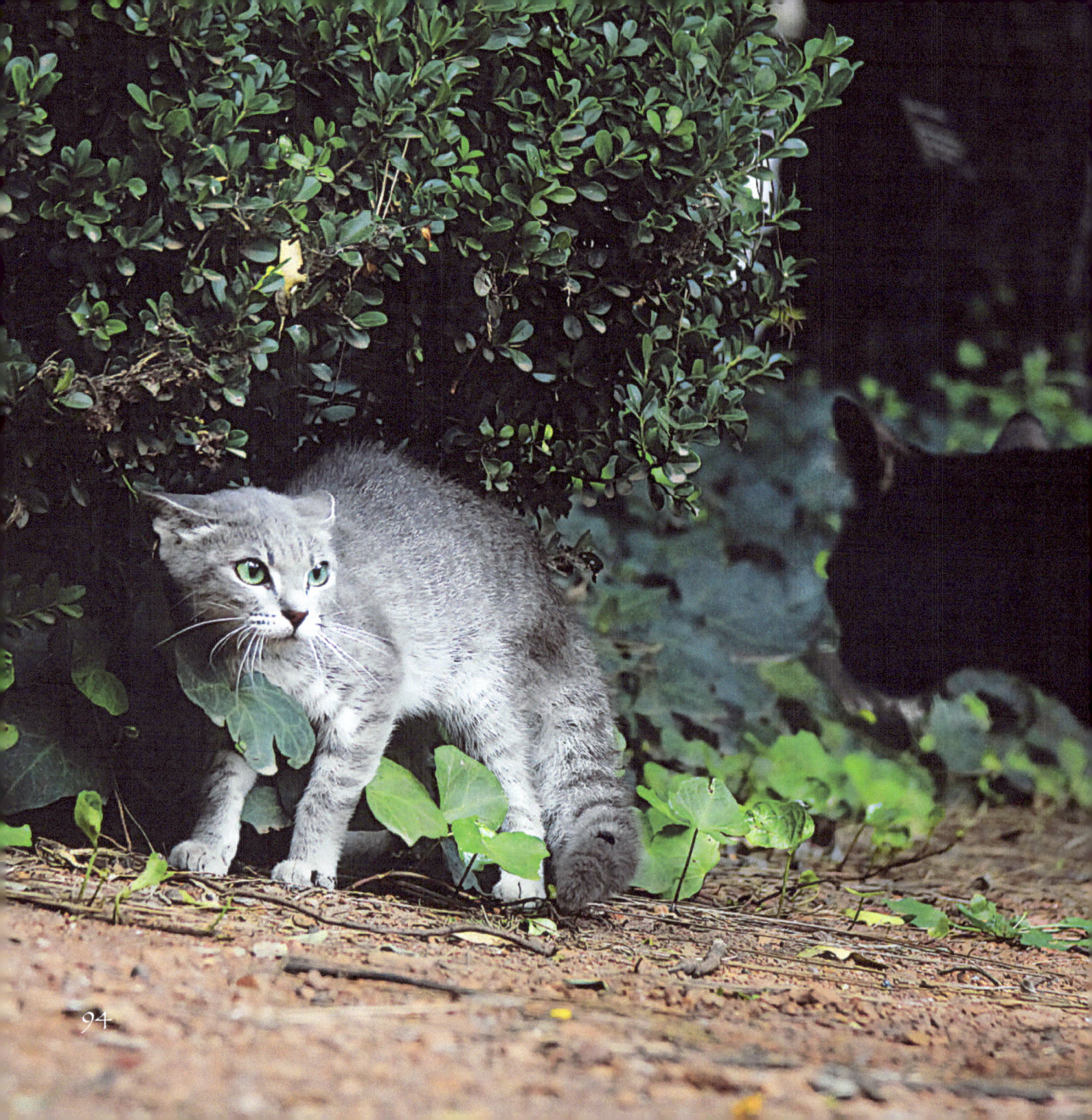

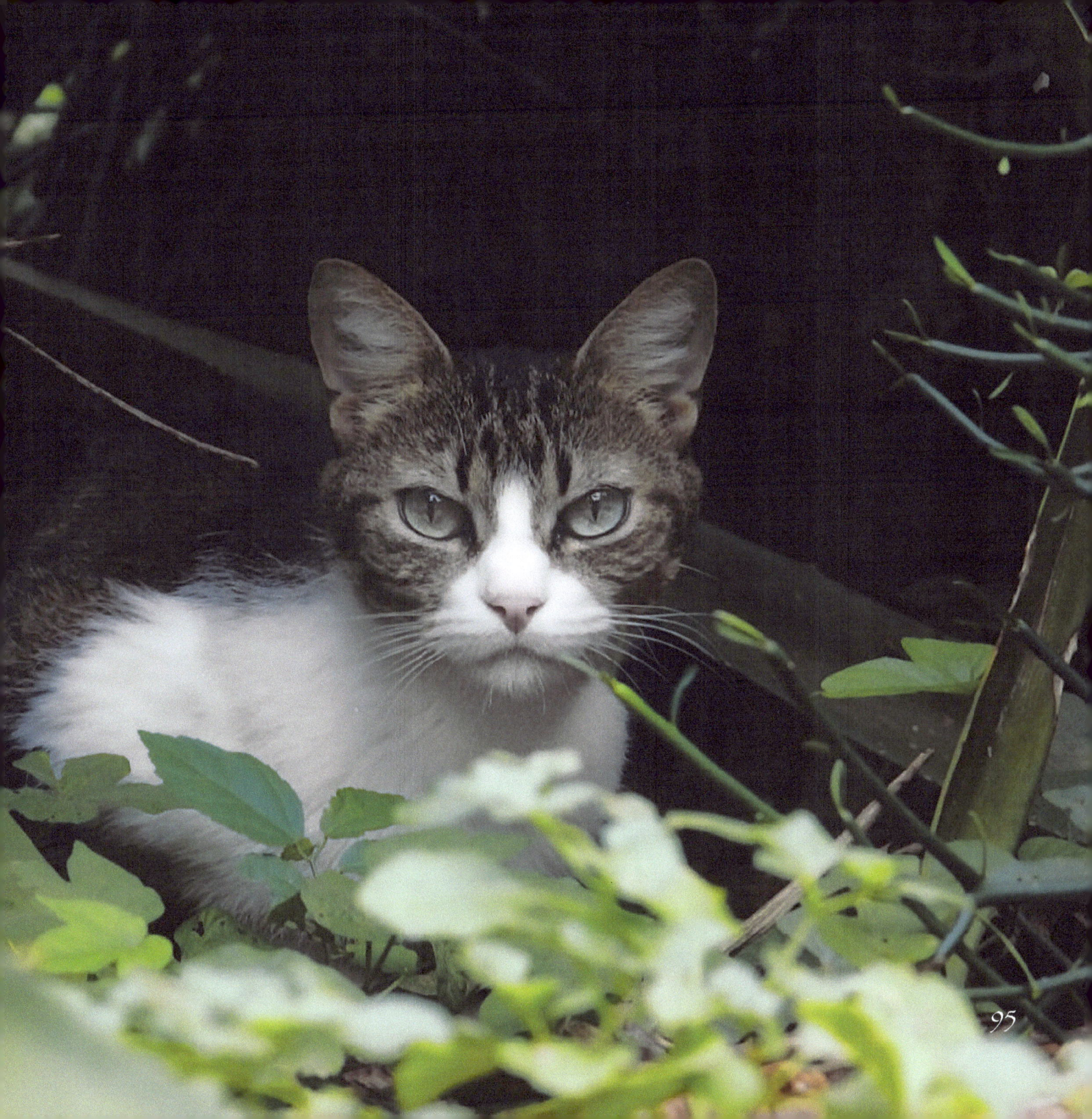

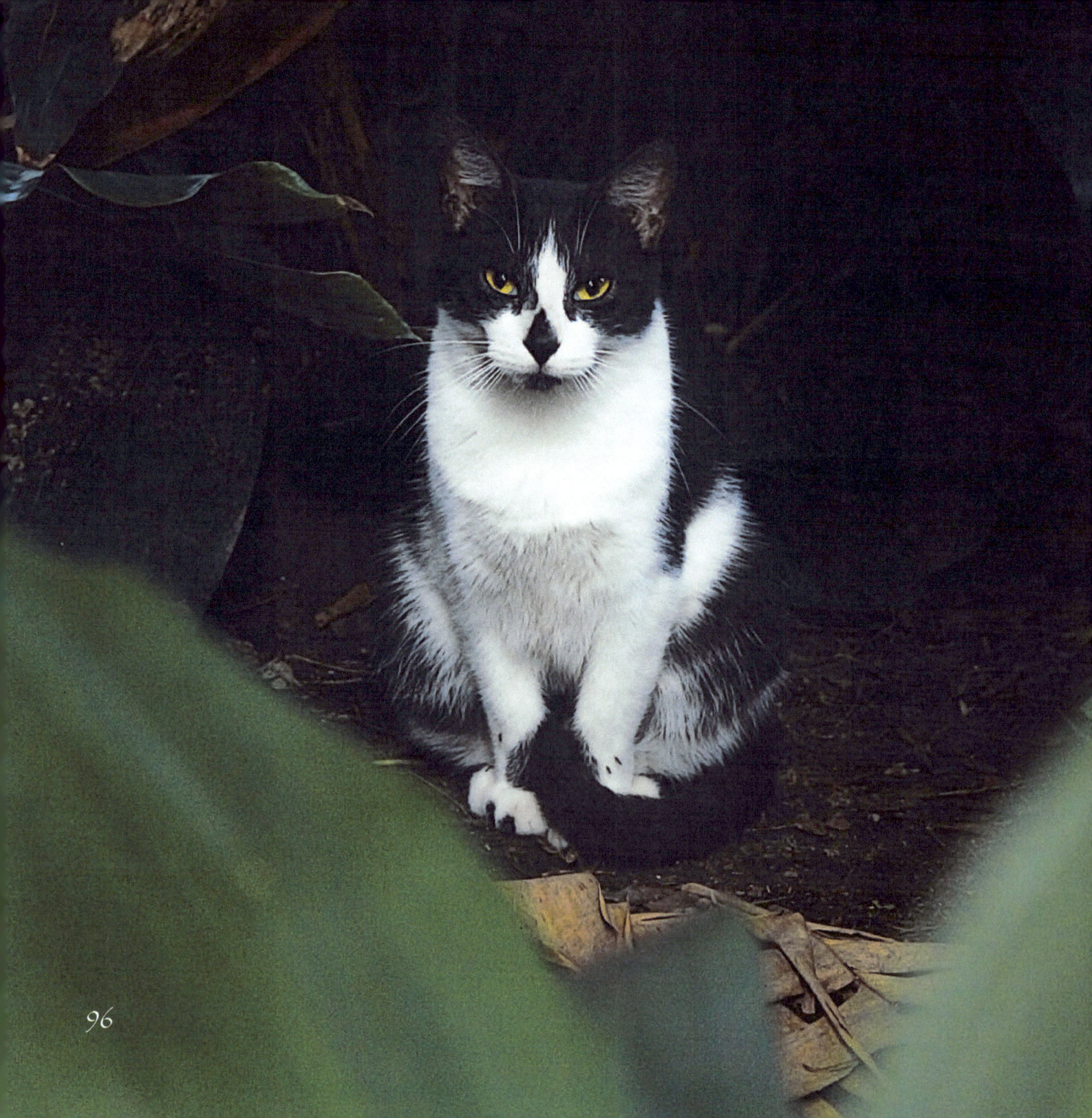

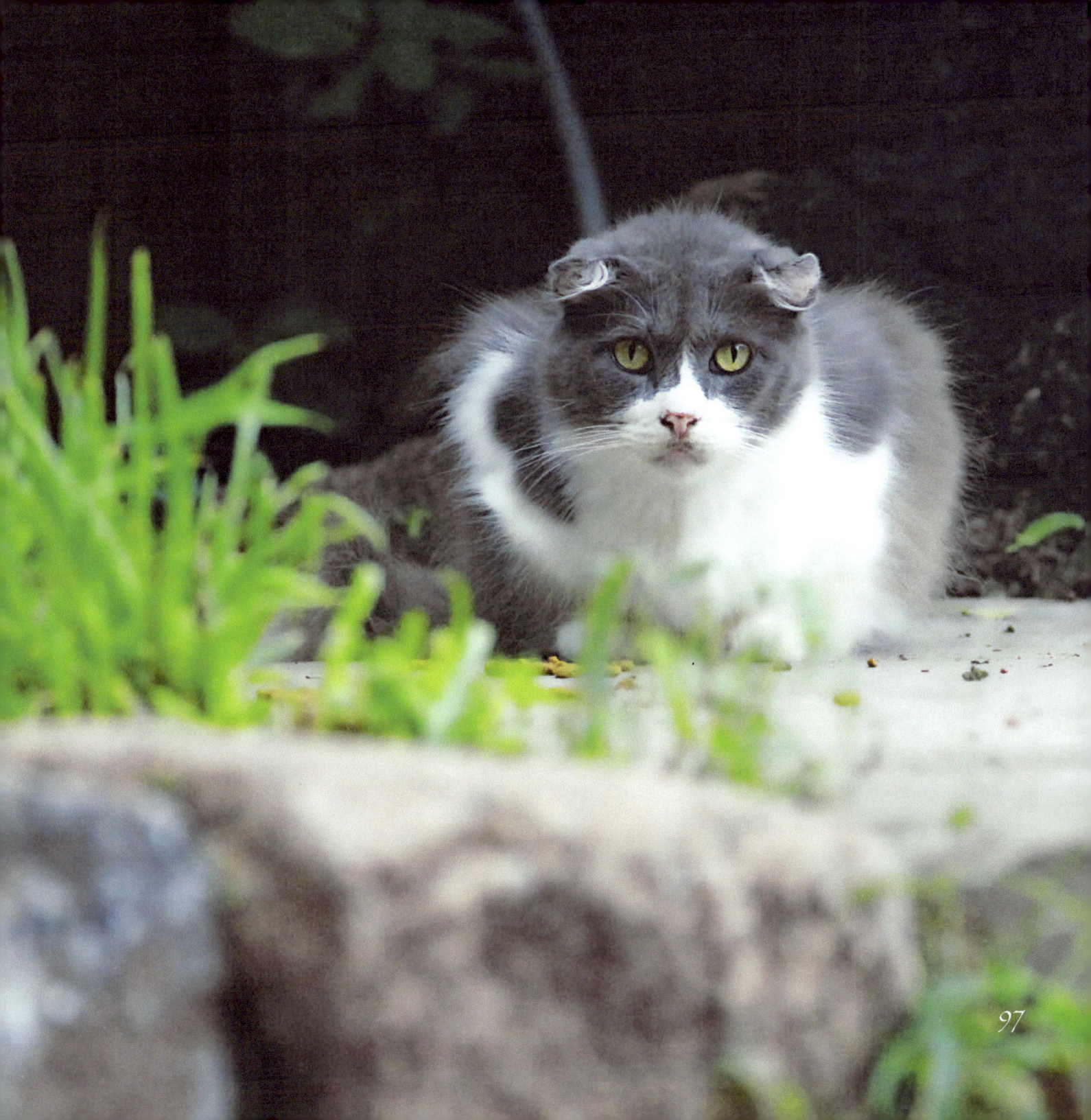

The average length of a cat's tail is between 9.9 and 11 inches

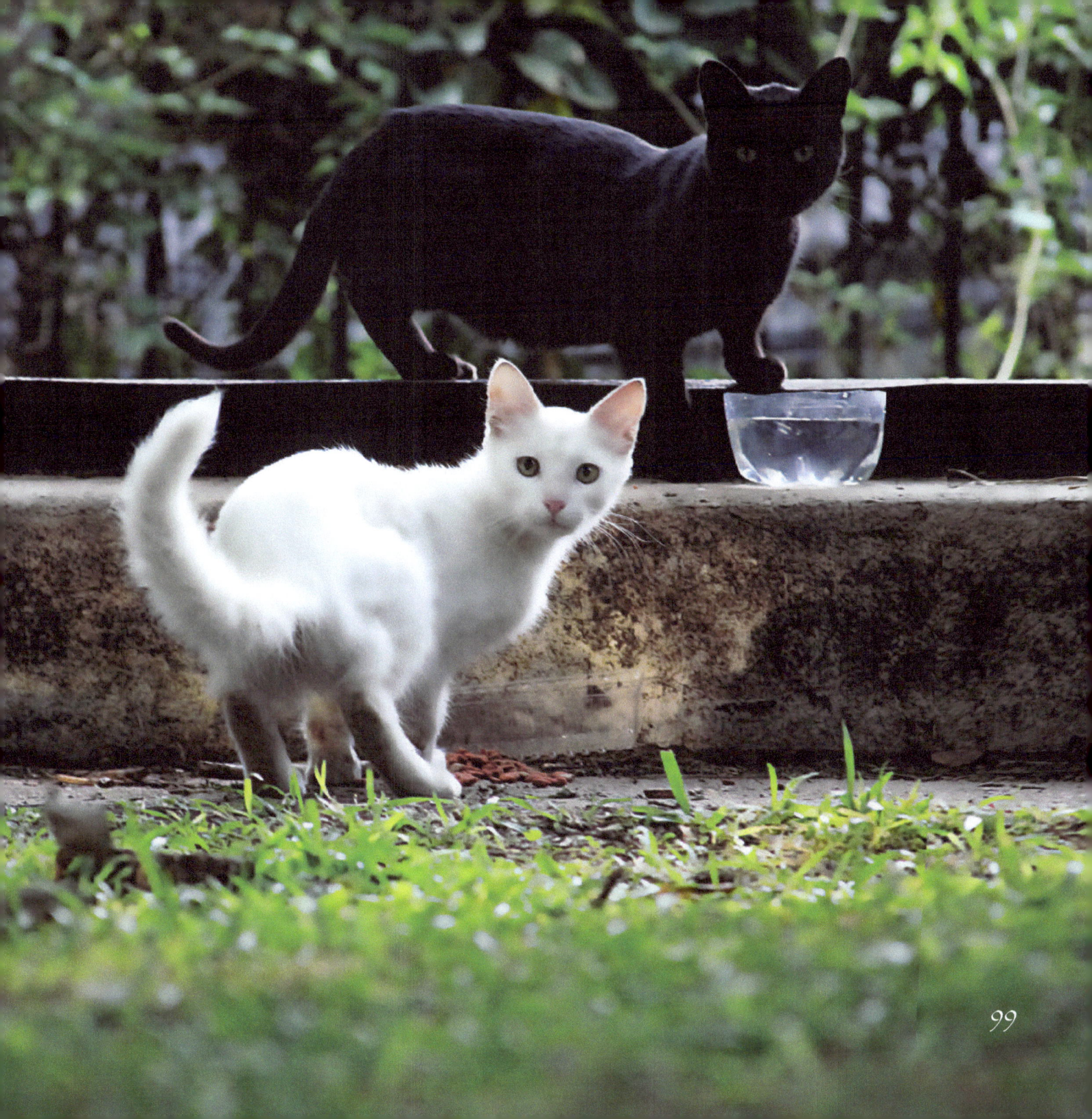

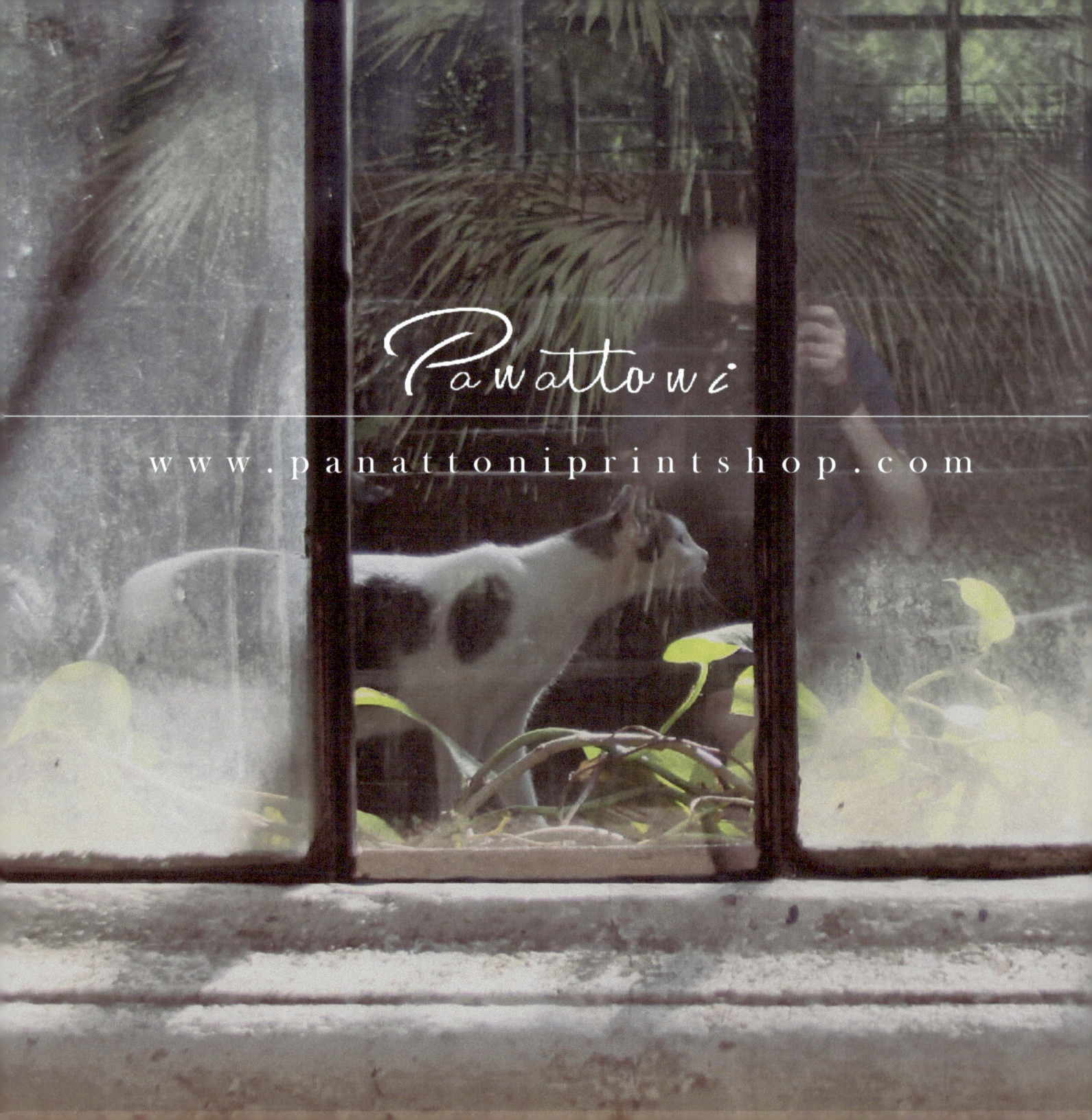

Panattoni

www.panattoniprintshop.com

www.ingramcontent.com/pod-product-compliance
Lightning Source LLC
Chambersburg PA
CBHW040323190526
45162CB00007B/56